Douglas Hyde

THE IRISH WRITERS SERIES
James F. Carens, General Editor

TITLE	*AUTHOR*
SEAN O'CASEY	Bernard Benstock
J. C. MANGAN	James Kilroy
W. R. RODGERS	Darcy O'Brien
STANDISH O'GRADY	Phillip L. Marcus
PAUL VINCENT CARROLL	Paul A. Doyle
SEUMAS O'KELLY	George Brandon Saul
SHERIDAN LEFANU	Michael Begnal
BRIAN FRIEL	D. E. S. Maxwell
DANIEL CORKERY	George Brandon Saul
EIMAR O'DUFFY	Robert Hogan
MERVYN WALL	Robert Hogan
FRANK O'CONNOR	James Matthews
JOHN BUTLER YEATS	Douglas Archibald
MARIA EDGEWORTH	James Newcomer
MARY LAVIN	Zack Bowen
SOMERVILLE AND ROSS	John Cronin
SUSAN L. MITCHELL	Richard M. Kain
J. M. SYNGE	Robin Skelton
KATHARINE TYNAN	Marilyn Gaddis Rose
LIAM O'FLAHERTY	James O'Brien
IRIS MURDOCH	Donna Gerstenberger
BENEDICT KIELY	Daniel J. Casey
DOUGLAS HYDE	Gareth Dunleavy
EDNA O'BRIEN	Grace Eckley
BRIAN MOORE	Jeanne Flood
ELIZABETH BOWEN	Edwin J. Kenney
JOHN MONTAGUE	Frank Kersnowski
CHARLES ROBERT MATURIN	Robert E. Lougy

GEORGE FITZMAURICE	Arthur E. McGuinness
FRANCIS STUART	J. H. Natterstad
PATRICK KAVANAGH	Darcy O'Brien
WILLIAM ALLINGHAM	Alan Warner
SIR SAMUEL FERGUSON	Malcolm Brown
LADY GREGORY	Hazard Adams
GEORGE RUSSELL (AE)	Richard M. Kain and James O'Brien
THOMAS DAVIS	Eileen Sullivan
PEADAR O'DONNELL	Grattan Freyer
OLIVER ST. JOHN GOGARTY	J. B. Lyons
SEUMAS HEANEY	Robert Buttel

Douglas Hyde

Gareth W. Dunleavy

WITHDRAWN

Lewisburg

BUCKNELL UNIVERSITY PRESS

London: Associated University Presses

© 1974 by Associated University Presses, Inc.

Associated University Presses, Inc.
Cranbury, New Jersey 08512

Associated University Presses
108 New Bond Street
London W1Y OQX, England

Library of Congress Cataloging in Publication Data

Dunleavy, Gareth W
  Douglas Hyde.
  (The Irish writers series)
  Bibliography: p.
  1. Hyde, Douglas, Pres. Irish Free State, 1860–1949.
I. Title.
DA965.H9D86   941.59'092'4 [B]   75–168805
ISBN 0–8387–7883–6
ISBN 0–8387–7975–1 (pbk.)

PRINTED IN THE UNITED STATES OF AMERICA

Contents

7

Acknowledgments

I record gratitude to the following among many:
Col. Thomas Manning, Ballyferriter, former military
aide to President Douglas Hyde; Captain T. McGlin-
chey, publisher to the Irish University Press, Dublin;
Mrs. Robert Holtby, wife of the Protestant rector
of Kilkeevan, Castlerea; Miss Josephine O'Conor,
Clonalis House, Castlerea; Michael 'O'Callaghan,
Editor, the Roscommon *Herald*; Séan Ó'Lúing, Dublin;
Peter Morrisroe, Bray; Mrs. Una Hyde Sealy, Dublin;
Miss Nora Niland, librarian and curator of the Sligo
Library and Museum; William Flynn, Boston, U.S.A.;
and to Bertie MacMaster, Kilmactranny, Pa Burke,
Castlerea, Bob Connolly, Portahard, Mrs. Kate Martin,
Kilmactranny, Miss Carrie Mahon and Mrs. Annie
Mahon, Frenchpark, perhaps the last of the splendid
company of old countrymen . . . and women!

For permission to quote from *Hail and Farewell*
I thank J. C. Medley and R. G. Medley, London,
copyright owners in George Moore. My thanks also
to Patrick Henchy, Director of the National Library of
Ireland for permission to quote extensively from unpublished Hyde manuscripts and correspondence; the

9

Macmillan Company for permission to quote from W. B. Yeats's *Autobiographies* (copyright 1916, 1936 by the Macmillan Company; renewed 1944 by Bertha Georgie Yeats); the Dr. Douglas Hyde Trust, and Irish University Press for permission to quote poems in whole and in part from *The Love Songs of Connacht* and *The Religious Songs of Connacht*.

To Janet Egleson Dunleavy, my wife and companion in all things Irish, I am indebted most for whatever is good in this little book.

Introduction

He told a startled Trinity lecturer that yes, he did know Greek, Latin, German, Hebrew, and French, but he dreamed in Irish. George Moore envied him his uncompromising dedication to the Irish language and Standish O'Grady stepped forward to silence Hyde's Trinity detractors by testifying that he knew the language as a living tongue. The poet Yeats decried the poet Hyde's role as a language propagandist but admitted that in fathering the Gaelic League, Hyde had done a job that he, Yeats, could never have done. Synge spoke up to assure that Hyde got proper credit for the first use of the Anglo-Irish dialect, and Lady Gregory said that by keeping the language alive, Hyde had kept Ireland alive.

On his American fund-raising tour of 1905–6 he had said: "We aim at a self-reliant, self-controlled, self-sufficient Ireland. We want to write our own books and our own songs, and to preserve our own dances. We want to go for nothing outside the four seas that can possibly be secured at home." And the crowds cheered, as they had at home, caught up in his fervor, and ready to forget that Hyde was both a Protestant and an intellectual. Douglas Hyde lived for the language and though it has been suggested that he fought a magnificent rearguard action for an already doomed cause, his achievement, actually a dual one, cannot be denied.

For in working to save the language Hyde had also rescued a body of folk literature that had been forced to the brink of oblivion by indifference, snobbery, intimidation, famine and fever. In saving that literature he gave a new resource to poets and playwrights determined to defy the encroachment of what Yeats had called "the stubborn uncomeliness of life." Theirs was already a world, observed Yeats, where nothing was allowed to become old and sacred and where powerful emotions were already being expressed in vulgar terms and symbols.

From Roscommon cottages and cabins where he had learned his first Irish from Aunt Anna, Seamus Hart, and Mrs. William Connally, from the storytellers who taught him to be a crack shot and angler; the poteen-drinkers and snuff-takers with the long Celtic memories who had survived the famine years, came tales and songs perilously close to extinction. *Beside the Fire* (1890), *Love Songs of Connacht* (1893), and *Religious, Songs of Connacht* (1906) were bilingual texts designed to make Irish easier to learn, and Hyde's prose translations and commentaries stirred the imaginations of hundreds who, Yeats felt, were in mortal danger of forever "talking like newspapers." These books were a boon for those who did not know Irish and who consequently had been barred from reading, memorizing, and reciting Hyde's own Irish poems that had circulated in the west and southwest for many seasons before 1893. To inform this fast-growing constituency about their literary and historical background, Hyde provided A *Literary History of Ireland* (1899), a pioneer work that, despite minor lapses, holds up well today. To open yet another avenue for development of the language, he turned to writing one-act plays in Irish for his Gaelic Leaguers. From his collaboration with Yeats and Lady Gregory on *Casadh an tSugan (The Twisting of the Rope), The Marriage, The Lost Saint,* and from Moore's help on *The Tinker and the Fairy,* Ireland received a second significant by-product of Hyde's crusade. By 1916 and the appearance of *Legends of Saints and Sinners,* his major literary achievement was behind him. Ahead lay scholarly writing, teaching at University College, Dublin until 1932, and a taxing second career as first President of Eire from 1938 to 1945.

Hyde has been meanly treated by some Irish poet-anthologists who owe him more than they have acknowledged publicly. Most of his books have been out of print for years. His Roscommon residence, "Ratra," close to his father's rectory and church at Portahard, Frenchpark, for years stood unroofed, another Big House stripped of its dignity, a symbol of the neglect shown its last occupant, who had returned it to its donor, the Gaelic League, on his death in 1949. In 1972 its walls were razed and the stone used as land fill for a new creamery in Ballaghaderreen.

Chronology

1860   Born 17 January, third son of Rev. Arthur Hyde, Jr., and Elizabeth Oldfield Hyde. Baptized in Protestant Church, Castlerea, Co. Roscommon, 11 March 1860. Baptismal register gives parents' residence as Kilmactranny, Co. Sligo, but birthplace was probably Castlerea, Co. Roscommon. Birthdate occasionally given incorrectly as 1862.

1867–80   Growing up in father's rectory at Frenchpark, Co. Roscommon. Taught at home and learned Irish from old country men and women with whom he associated.

1879–82   First poems, mostly in Irish, published in *The Shamrock*. Adopts pseudonym *An Craoibhin Aoibhin* ("The delightful little branch").

1880   Enters Trinity College, Dublin.

1881   Wins Bedell Scholarship at TCD given to future preachers in Irish.

1884   B.A., Trinity College. Wins gold medal in modern literature.

1885–86   Original poems in Irish and two essays published in *Dublin University Review*.

1886   Wins special Theology prize. Transfers to law school.

1886 Ll.D., Trinity College, Dublin.

1889 *Leabhar Sgealaigheachta,* first volume of folktales, published.

1890 *Beside the Fire,* collection of folktales, published.

1891 One-year appointment as professor of modern languages in University of New Brunswick.

1892 "The Necessity for De-Anglicising Ireland," inaugural lecture as President of the National Literary Society.

1893 *Love Songs of Connacht* published. Marries Lucy Kurtz (d. 1938). Assumes presidency of Gaelic League at its founding.

1895 *The Three Sorrows of Story-Telling* published.
The Story of Early Gaelic Literature published.

1898 Meets Lady Gregory for the first time.

1899 *A Literary History of Ireland* published. Works at Coole Park on *Casadh an tSugan (Twisting of the Rope)* with W. B. Yeats.

1901 *Twisting of the Rope* performed in Irish at Gaiety Theatre, Dublin, October 21. First Irish play produced in any theater.

1902 *The Marriage* (play). Collaborates with Lady Gregory in writing of this play.

1903 Hyde works on plays at Coole Park in summer.
The Tinker and the Fairy (play).
The Lost Saint (play).
Songs Ascribed to Raftery published.

1905–6 Makes American tour on behalf of Gaelic League.

1906 *The Religious Songs of Connacht* published.

1909 Appointed to chair of modern Irish at University College, Dublin.

1911   *The Nativity Play.*

1915   After revolutionaries take over the Gaelic League, Hyde resigns its presidency which he had held for twenty-one years.

1916   *Legends of Saints and Sinners* published.
Death of daughter Nuala, of consumption.

1917   *The Conquests of Charlemagne* published.

1918   *Catalogue of Books and Manuscripts in the Gilbert Collection* published.

1925   Senator in Irish Senate. Summers spent at "Ratra" near Frenchpark, home purchased and given to Hyde by Gaelic League.

1932   Retires from chair at University College, Dublin, to live at "Ratra."

1937   *Mo Turus go hAmerice* published. Hyde's account of his American tour.
Mise agus an Connradh published. Hyde's account of his part in the Gaelic League.

1938–45   Serves as first President of Eire.

1939   *Mayo Stories told by Thomas Casey* published.

1940   Suffers stroke followed by semi-invalidism.

1949   July 12. Dies in Phoenix Park residence, Dublin. Buried in graveyard of Protestant Church, Portahard, near Frenchpark.

Douglas Hyde

The Company of Old Countrymen

In the twenty-second summer since his death on July 12, 1949, there were still "old ones" scattered through the hillside and crossroad parishes of Sligo and Roscommon whose powerful memories recalled Douglas Hyde. Some were the grandchildren of the "hewers of wood and drawers of water" who had been young Hyde's tutors in the Gaelic language and lore, whom he called "the last Milesians" to distinguish them from the others, "the undertakers, planters and colonists of the Anglo-Irish gentry."

At Kilmactranny, an obscure County Sligo village between Loughs Arrow and Skean, only eight miles from Boyle in County Roscommon, stands the church where the Reverend Arthur Hyde Jr. was Protestant vicar until 1867 and where Douglas Hyde probably spent the first seven years of his life.

For Kate McDonagh Martin, the former Kilmactranny rectory has been home for over forty years. She repeated the local tradition that Douglas Hyde was not born there because his mother Elizabeth, daughter of the Reverend Archdeacon John Oldfield, Protestant rector at Castlerea, County Roscommon, had gone to her father's home, "The Hill", to have her third son. Standard biographies incorrectly give Frenchpark, midway between Boyle and Castlerea as Hyde's birthplace. The Kilmactranny tradition is partially corroborated in the *Register of Baptisms* for 1860 in the Protestant parish of Kilkeevan, Castlerea. The entry for a baptism performed on 11 March 1860, gives the child's name as Douglas Hyde; his birthdate is noted as 17 January 1860, his parents' names are listed as Arthur and Bessy, and their residence is given as Kilmactranny. The entry also states that Arthur Hyde performed the baptism of his third son, Douglas. Given the inaccessibility of Kilmactranny in 1860 and the primitive condition of roads, particularly during winter rains, it is unlikely that Arthur and Elizabeth Hyde took their two-months-old son by carriage the thirty miles to Castlerea for baptism. It is more probable that Elizabeth Hyde went to her father's spacious home in Castlerea in November or December 1859, had her child in his house in January, and returned to Kilmactranny with her husband and son in the spring of 1860.

Kilmactranny was a primitive and remote area with few native Irish speakers in 1860. Bertie MacMaster's father, born there in 1848, told his son that in his youth, two old women living down the rutted dirt road were the only Irish speakers, and in MacMaster's own lifetime there have been no native Irish speakers in the parish. Douglas Hyde's first contact with the language whose cause he championed vigorously to the end of his life came in those years after the family's removal to Frenchpark in 1867 and before his enrollment as a student in the Divinity Curriculum at Trinity College in 1880. That he never went back to Kilmactranny is most likely explained by the extinction of Irish there. Hyde's intense efforts to hear and write down Gaelic tales from Irish speakers in Roscommon, Galway, and Sligo would have been wasted in Kilmactranny. Kate Martin tells, however, of a Kilmactranny youth who found himself facing Hyde as his examiner in Irish at Galway. Thomas Condon understood the first question put to him in Irish by Hyde, "Where are you from?" When he replied "Kilmactranny," Hyde switched immediately to English, much to young Condon's relief, and questioned him closely about people and places in the village.

Kilmactranny was the first of a score of locales, all within thirty miles of one another, rich in traditions and sites associated with Ireland's prehistory and history that Douglas Hyde would come to know intimately in his first twenty years. His Greek, Latin, and Hebrew were learned in his father's rectory, "the Glebe house" at Frenchpark, but his Irish tutors were the old women of the bog huts and men like the venerable Fenian, Johnny Lavin, and a neighbor's gamekeeper, James Hart. These boyhood friends filled Hyde with tales and legends laced with allusions to places in easy walking and cycling range. It was his detailed firsthand knowledge of the Sligo and Roscommon countryside's artifacts and personages, real and fictional, coupled with his quickness for the Irish language that made Hyde's *Literary History of Ireland* so impressive on its publication in 1899. He had walked the Moytura townlands that preserve the name of Magh Tuireadh, the Plain of Pillars, where tradition said the two great battles had occurred in which the Tuatha De Danaan defeated the Fomorians.

About Kilmactranny still stand a profusion of pillar stones, gallery graves, chamber tombs, dolmens, and an ancient stone cross. Nearby are the remains of Shancoe where St. Patrick founded a church and where lived the eminent seventeenth-century scribe Lame David Duignan. Close by is Mounttown, formerly Knockmore, the birthplace of the eighteenth-century scholar-antiquarian Charles O'Conor of Belanagare.

On the road from Kilmactranny to Frenchpark and Castlerea lay Boyle, a town famous for its twelfth-century abbey whose patrons had been the O'Conors, O'Haras, and the Mac Dermotts of Moylurg, famous families of medieval Connacht. There was buried the thirteenth-century bard O'Daly and from the monastery on nearby Trinity Island in Lough Key had come the important *Annals of Loch Cé*. On Lough Key's south shore lay the demesne of Rockingham, its magnificent house burned down for the first time in 1863. In the middle of Lough Key were the remains of the Castle of the Mac Dermott of Moylurg, which seized W. B. Yeats's imagination when in 1896 Hyde had taken him there. The poet saw in it his "Castle of Heroes," a proper shrine where he could organize a new form of worship and a mystical order for Ireland. North from Boyle ran the winding road to Ballinafad and Sligo, passing through the Curlews, where in 1599 the Irish under Red Hugh O'Donnell had thrown back the English under Sir Conyers Clifford. West of Ballinafad in the heart of the Bricklieve mountains is the Bronze Age village site of Carrowkeel with its many chamber tombs and the footings of nearly fifty circular huts. Less than ten miles to the northwest is Ballymote, where close to 1400 the *Book of Ballymote* was compiled. Hyde's reliance on it for genealogical and literary evidence is reflected in his *Literary History of Ireland.*

Sixteen miles south of Boyle is Elphin, significant in the ecclesiastical history of Connacht since St. Patrick had established a bishopric there in the fifth century. In his chapter on the Ossianic poems in the *Literary History,* Hyde tells how he had listened to Roscommon stories of Ossian's meeting with St. Patrick when drawing stones at Elphin.

Nineteen miles southwest of Boyle is Castlerea, the town of Hyde's baptism and the birthplace of Sir William Wilde, the oculist and antiquary who was the poet's father. Just west of the town is Clonalis House, the seat of O'Conor Don, head of the O'Conors of Connacht, former ruling family of the Province. In later years Hyde would often visit Clonalis to examine its Gaelic manuscripts and join the shooting parties on its grounds.

In Tulsk, only ten miles from Frenchpark and the Protestant rectory where Hyde lived until 1880, lay the Rathcroghan group of antiquities. Here young Hyde could see the supposed residence of "Queen" Medb of the *Táin Bo Cuailnge,* walk over Carnfree, the inauguration ground of the ancient Connacht kings, and touch the supposed burial stone of Dathi, last pagan king of Ireland. Nearby, at the tumulus of Dumha Shealga, associated in literature with early Connacht royalty, was to be seen the outline of still-buried evidence supporting the legends told in the cottages and preserved in blackened, dog-eared manuscripts, some of which Hyde would save from destruction.

The years of growing in Roscommon imbued Douglas Hyde with fierce respect for that long Celtic memory for things unwritten. As a young man he often passed through the doorway of Bridget Crummy's hut in the bog to seat himself beside the turf fire and spinning wheel and take her tea brewed in the one blackened saucepan that served also as a teapot. From Biddy Crummy, recalled today as "wonderful at the Irish," Hyde heard the stanzas of "Mo brón air an bfairrge" ("My Grief on the Sea") which he would print in 1893 in *Love Songs of Connacht (Abhráin Grádh Chúige Connacht)*.

In his boyhood diaries, begun in 1874 at the age of fourteen, Hyde tried his hand at writing Irish, describing his chats with Seamus Hart, his rambles across the bogs, and his adventures with his brothers, all in a peculiar phonetic spelling. Gradually he turned to writing in Gaelic script, using as his chief aid the Reverend William Neilson's *Introduction to the Irish Language,* printed in 1843 primarily for the use of Protestant missionaries in Irish-speaking areas. By 1877 he was writing fiercely anti-English verses in Irish and in his diary he noted the success of a Fenian meeting held in Frenchpark on February 25, 1877.

From Seamus Hart Hyde first heard the legend of the *alp-luachra* (newt) and how a wealthy Connacht farmer had been afflicted by the creature to the point where only Mac Dermott, Prince of Coolavin on Lough Gara—"the best doctor in Connacht or the five provinces"—could save him. This story, recreated in Hyde's *Cois na Teine (Beside the Fire)* of 1890, is accompanied by a note crediting Hart as being "one of the best reciters I ever met."

Seamus Hart, Martin Brennan, Walter Sherlock, and

others to whom he listened as a youth in Roscommon Hyde would describe in the preface to *Beside the Fire* as representative of "the oldest, most neglected, and poorest of the Irish-speaking population." By 1890 he would write that almost all of his informants, half-starving Connacht cottagers, were dead: "Ten or fifteen years ago I used to hear a great many stories, but I did not understand their value. Now when I go back for them I cannot find them. They have died out and will never again be heard on the hillsides, where they probably existed for a couple of thousand years; they will never be repeated here again, to use the Irish phrase, while grass grows or water runs."

The disciplining of his enthusiasm for the language and legends alive in his youth in the Roscommon cottages led Hyde to international prominence as a folklorist—the ablest in a line that had begun with T. Crofton Croker in 1825 and included Patrick Kennedy, Lady Wilde, and the American, Jeremiah Curtin. But Roscommon also deserved credit for Hyde's ascendancy to the front rank of Irish cultural nationalism by 1893, for it was the old Roscommon Fenian, Johnny Lavin, who first raised young Hyde's contempt for his countrymen who eagerly accepted the tongue of an alien and oppressive culture. In 1890, at age thirty, he jabbed sharply in *Beside the Fire* at "those men who for the last sixty years have had the ear of the race [and who] have persistently shown the cold shoulder to everything that was Irish and racial, and while protesting, or pretending to protest, against West Britonism, have helped, more than anyone else, by their example to assimilate us to England and things English."

Hyde was a fiery, albeit secret, nationalist when he left Frenchpark for Trinity College in 1880 at the age of twenty. His student commonplace book with entries that run to 1882 has recently been acquired by the National Library. In it are notes on history and literature written in German, Latin, and English, often in a hand using Irish characters. Scattered among the young schollar's notes are his miscellaneous patriotic poems. One he composed in four-line stanzas in honor of the Fenian leader, O'Donovan Rossa:

> But English gold as ever of old
> Betrayed the rightful cause,
> And English spies and lies
> And bloody English laws.

> And the dungeon clay was Rossa's bed,
> Cold and damp and bare,
> And the people were left without a head
> And broken was their war.

In another perfervid patriotic poem written probably immediately before his departure from Frenchpark for Dublin in 1880, young Hyde celebrates one of Ireland's abortive revolutions:

> When in its full intensity
> A patriot spirit burned,
> That clung to what was native
> And what was foreign spurned.
> . . . .
> Then fire upon fire
> On every hilltop high
> In Leinster, Meath and Connacht

> Rose red into the sky.
> That was no smouldering fire
> Of artificial flame,
> The fuel was a nation,
> The match was Freedom's name.

The prevailing image of Douglas Hyde in post–1916 Ireland has been of a man who relied only on moral suasion and foreswore force and violence; who was dedicated solely to a reanimation of the ethnic spirit of his country; who was dedicated only to making his country intellectually interesting, not politically free of British shackles; who was selected as Ireland's first president because he was "above the struggle." But when the inevitable reappraisal of this over-simplified view is made, it is almost certain that Hyde will emerge as a man who showed deeper, more subtle and timely responses to his country's needs than some of his more colorful contemporaries.

The fiery young Trinity undergraduate from Roscommon came under the influence of a powerful personality midway in his Trinity years. John O'Leary had returned to Dublin in 1884 from five years of British imprisonment and exile in France for his part in the 1867 Fenian rising. For Hyde, Yeats, Katherine Tynan, Maude Gonne, and other young nationalists, O'Leary was *the* veteran patriot and they flocked to him. But O'Leary decried violence—"there are things that a man must not do to save a nation"—and instead pressed for the building of what he called the national morale. Pessimistic about Ireland's chances for early independence and strong in his hatred not so much for England as for English rule in Ireland, O'Leary preached basically unpolitical precepts: first that an Irishman should feel that he was an Irishman; second, that Irish unity must be secured; and third, that each man should make some sacrifice for Ireland. There seems little doubt that O'Leary's philosophy was embraced and followed by Hyde for the remainder of his life.

After 1884, the Hyde of the schoolboy patriotic poems became a disciplined and practical realist working to raise the Irish cultural conscience. This he achieved most notably through his leadership of the Gaelic League for twenty-one years after its founding in 1893. That by 1923 he fairly understood the role the League had played in bringing about Irish independence is clear in his essay first printed in the *Manchester Guardian* and reprinted in John Devoy's *Gaelic American* of August 11: " . . . the movement which has resulted in the establishment of our Government is the descendant of the Gaelic League, and the Gaelic League goes back to Gaelic Ireland, to ancient Ireland for its inspiration. The Gaelic League grew up and became the spiritual father of Sinn Fein, and Sinn Fein's progeny were the Volunteers, who forced the English to make the treaty. The Dail is the child of the Volunteers, and thus it descends directly from the Gaelic League, whose traditions it inherits. . . ."

In possession of the National Library of Ireland is a manuscript in Hyde's hand with the date 7 October 1883 inscribed on its last page. This is a remarkably revealing dream allegory of 194 pages completed three years after Hyde's enrollment in the divinity curriculum at Trinity and only two years after he had won the Bedell scholarship for future preachers in Irish. In it he writes of feeling "unwell and uneasy" after a night of drinking illicit whiskey (poteen) and then wondering whether it was right to indulge in what the government had forbidden. He then quickly satisfied himself by his reflection "that the government not being a native or self-chosen one, its orders could not be allowed to be valid" (p. 1). He goes on to ponder on the doctrine of "rendering unto Caesar the things that are Caesar's" and "St. Paul's admonition that one ought to endure the state he's in, and not seek violently to alter it." This line of thought brought on a headache and he decided to fish upon a lake that was "broad and lonely" (Lough Gara, near Frenchpark?). Falling asleep in his boat, he had a "remarkable dream that left rather a deep and vivid impression behind it."

He dreamt that as he walked with his Conscience and Reason, Conscience proposed that they all live together in his house. Hyde concurred when "Reason said he would be the servant and Conscience said I should be the host." A Jew and a Mohammedan visited the house and told Hyde he should choose a religion. They were accompanied by a gentleman dressed in black "who . . . had served my family so well that both my grandfathers were in receipt of some £800 a year, thanks to him, during the greater part of their lives . . . and he had taken care that their office should be a comparative sinecure." The disparaging allusion here is to the vocation of Hyde's grandfathers who, like his father, were clergymen who had looked after the spiritual needs of Ascendancy households since the Hyde family's arrival in Cork from Berkshire in the reign of Elizabeth. Now young Hyde at twenty-three feared he was destined to follow suit, and was deeply troubled at the prospect.

Shortly, a new character, Mr. Nogod, was introduced in the dream (p. 22). He identified himself as the representative of atheism and presented Hyde with books including the *Critique of Pure Reason, Leviathan,* and *The Rights of Man* with the advice that he begin by reading the last—"that is lively and will lay a foundation." Hyde was next visited by a Chinese and his earlier visitors mail him notes asking for second interviews. Hyde felt that he should read his books before granting a second interview to those who sought to convert him to their respective faiths. A long second interview with Nogod followed in which Hyde was told: "Religion is only another name for party. Religion and politics are the two great sources of nearly all the quarrels social and domestic, the two great causes of all the strife and embittered feelings of the world, the two fruitful springs of pain and cruelty and heart-scalding all over this earth, and of the two religion does the most harm. Can you deny it?"

Hyde answered Nogod falteringly, saying "there is more or less truth in what you say," and went on to declare that he thought the misery of the world "lay in the villainous nature of man, and not so much in the fact of his having religion or no religion." When Reason was asked by Nogod whether he detected flaws in his argument for atheism, Hyde wrote: "Reason remained silent, apparently because he could think of nothing to say." An argument then ensued between the parson and Nogod. Hyde noted ironically that it was difficult to tell whether the individual he called parson might not be a priest: "I never could tell which" (p: 99). While the parson continued his argument with the atheist, a final offer arrived from the Hyde family's old friend, the "gentleman dressed in black."

Dear Mr. Hyde,
    I have a rather good position vacant just now if you care to accept it. As matters go, it is not bad in a monetary point of view, and payments are regular. There is a good house attached, and the farm—contains 30 English acres of good arable land. . . . P.S. I forgot to mention that the work is practically nil.

At this point the dream allegory ended as Hyde's boat that had drifted to the opposite shore of the lake struck a stone; he awakened to hear himself say, "I will think about it."

Hyde had entered Trinity with the apparent intent of following his father, grandfather, and great-grandfather into the Protestant ministry. But the skepticism for the clergy reflected in the unpublished dream allegory of 1883 ran deep and was to emerge later in the preface to his *Story of Early Gaelic Literature* (1895) where Hyde commented acidly on "the exclusively few out of the hordes of English clerical placemen of the seventeenth and eighteenth centuries who attempted either to understand the country and its people, or to give back something for all they took." Significantly, in his six years in the Trinity divinity curriculum, he won numerous prizes for his Irish prose and verse, but after winning a special theology prize in 1886, he transferred to the law school. After his first appearance in print with poems in *The Shamrock* (1879), he contributed during those Trinity years more poems, mostly in Irish, to that magazine, and wrote an original poem in Irish and two prose articles

for the *Dublin University Review*. In 1888, his last year at
Trinity, he took his law degree and contributed along
with Yeats, Rolleston, and others to *Poems and Ballads of
Young Ireland*. The next year saw the publication of his
first collection of folktales, *Leabhar Sgealaigheachta*. By
then, all the doubts raised in the 1883 allegory were fully
resolved. Hyde was a dedicated folkllorist and a declared
Irish Irelander.

W. B. Yeats, in his artistically rearranged *Autobiography*, chose to see Hyde as a slightly eccentric rustic
poseur, "a very dark young man, who filled me with
surprise, partly because he had pushed a snuff-box
toward me. . . . I . . . set him down as a peasant, and
wondered what brought him to college, and to a Protestant college. . . . " With some slight condescension,
Yeats commented on Hyde's taste for snuff, poteen, and
his fluency in the Irish language, all due, said Yeats, to
Hyde's frequenting "the company of old countrymen."
He went on to pay somewhat grudging tribute to Hyde's
popularity as a Gaelic poet whose verses vere picked up
from the newspapers where he had published them
under the name "Craoibhin Aoibhin" (Little Branch)
and sung, said Yeats, by "mowers and reapers from
Donegal to Kerry." It was Hyde, Yeats conceded, who
had sent him the manuscript of the "best tale in my
Faery and Folk Tales." Yeats dimly recalled that he had
something to do with the London publication of Hyde's
Beside the Fire and did praise that collection for having
the "beautiful English of Connaught, which is Gaelic
in idiom and Tudor in vocabulary." But, said Yeats of
Hyde, "the harps and the pepperpots got him" and "I
mourn for the greatest folklorist who ever lived and for

the young poet who died in his youth." Nevertheless, Yeats admited, "He was to create a great popular movement (the Gaelic League), far more important in its practical results than any movement I could have made."

In sharp contrast to Yeats's condescending appraisal of Hyde's "uncritical folk genius" is the respect paid young Hyde's role in the Irish language movement by a contemporary, William Larminie. He had joined Yeats's Irish Literary Society in London and its counterpart in Dublin and recognized Hyde as already influential in the struggle to keep Irish alive. At least twice Larminie wrote to Hyde arguing for the adoption of a simplified phonetic spelling if Irish were to survive. In the first letter, dated 12 January 1888, Larminie wrote: "It will be impossible to teach the peasantry to read the present spelling in addition to English. The latter is difficult and troublesome enough. Irish is worse. But as English will be a necessity, Irish unless made easy, will inevitably go." Again, on February 22, he writes: "Either you make up your mind that the language cannot be kept alive:—if this is so the one thing you can do for it is to *study* it while it is alive under all its varieties and place them on record: this cannot be done if they are all covered up under a delusive appearance of uniformity . . . *OR* you believe that the language may be kept alive; and in this case you are confronted by the question whether the only efficient means of keeping it living is not to free it from the burden of its antiquated and inefficient orthography." Although the challenge to survival of Irish posed by its spelling was apparent to Hyde from his first contact with it, he felt unable to follow Larminie's advice in *Leabhar Sgealaigheachta,* his first collection of Irish folktales, published in 1889.

In a manuscript held by the National Library of Ireland dated Christmas, 1889, and bearing the title "Essay on Irish Folklore," Hyde lamented the death of Irish on Achill Island "when a few words by Michael Davitt or Tim Healy . . . next time they got to Achill would be quite sufficient to keep Irish alive there." Parts of this essay seem to have supplied material for the preface to *Beside the Fire.* Hyde gave his formula for successfully capturing the shanachies' stories: half a glass of whiskey ("a whole glass generally puts them off their heads") and a pipe of tobacco; patience to listen through without an interrupting word and then to say "I wish I had that on paper." He recorded that he had "some 20 or 30 stories, some of which I published in Irish with copious notes, and more of which I am going to publish in English and Irish."

On his return from a one-year interim professorship at the University of New Brunswick in 1891, Hyde assumed the presidency of the National Literary Society. His inaugural lecture, "The Necessity for De-Anglicising Ireland," given in November, 1892, has been called his most famous and most fruitful lecture. Donal McCartney's admirable summary of it is in his essay "Hyde, D. P. Moran and Irish Ireland," in *Leaders and Men of the Easter Rising* (1967): "Hyde held that the Irish, once one of the most cultural nations in Europe, were now one of the least so, and that this state of affairs had been brought about by Anglicization. By giving up the native language and customs the Irish had thrown away with a light heart the best claim which they had upon the world's recognition as a separate nation. What, asked Hyde, did Mazzini say?—That the Irish ought to be content as an integral part of the United Kingdom because they had lost the notes of nationality. While, said Hyde, the Irish claimed to hate the English yet they imitated them in dress, literature, music, games and ideas, only a long time after them and a long way behind. But at the bottom of the Irish heart was the Gaelic past which prevented them from becoming citizens of the Empire. In order to de-Anglicize, the Irish would have to create a strong feeling against West-Britonism and arrest at once the decay of the language. For this purpose nothing less than a house to house visitation and exhortation of the people would do. The soul of Ireland was to be rediscovered *not* in the descendants of the Cromwellians and Williamites who sat in Grattan's Parliament, but said Hyde, in the descendants of the hewers of wood and drawers of water, the ordinary people themselves."

In 1893, on the suggestion of Eoin MacNeill and largely as a result of Hyde's fierce propaganda in behalf of the language, the Gaelic League was formed with Hyde as its president. Thirty years later in an essay for the *Manchester Guardian* entitled "The Irish Language Movement: Some Reminiscences" (reprinted in Devoy's *Gaelic American*) Hyde traced the reasons for the virtual extinction of Irish in the nineteenth century, the rise of various societies dedicated to preserving it, and the background to the forming of the Gaelic League and the success with which its efforts were met. With great tact and skill, Hyde had organized and directed a popular campaign to keep Irish alive where it was spoken and to encourage its acceptance for its own sake elsewhere in Ireland. The patriotic fervor of his early Trinity years had been exchanged for an image of moderacy, restraint, and conciliation during his presidency of the Gaelic League. All these qualities served him well until 1915 when he was defeated by the Sinn Fein revolutionaries in the League on the issue of whether the League should stand for a "free Ireland." Hyde's strategy for the League until that year was outlined by him in a passage from an unpublished history quoted in Myles Dillon's essay on Hyde in *The Shaping of Modern Ireland*:

> I am not at all sure that the turn things have taken may not be the best thing for the language movement. It has put an end to my dream of using the language as a unifying bond to join all Irishmen together, but it at least rendered the movement homogeneous. . . . It is quite possible that it may prove that the language has been best served by the extreme party confiscating it for themselves as their own particular asset.
>
> My own ideas had been quite different. My ambition had always been to use the language as a neutral field upon which all Irishmen might meet. . . . We were doing the only business that really counted, we were keeping Ireland Irish. . . . So long as we remained non-political, there was no end to what we could do. But the moment we became political, all the significance of the movement as one to build up a nation from all classes and creeds came to an end.
>
> I am not at all sure that the League did not do the right thing for the language in practically throwing me over. I did not see this at the time, however, for I did not foresee the utter and swift débacle of the Irish Parliamentary Party and the apotheosis of Sinn Féin. The only reason I had for keeping politics out was the desire to offend no-

body and get help from every party, which I did. But when Sinn Féin swallowed up all parties except the Unionists this was no longer necessary.

In 1893, the same year of the Gaelic League's founding, Hyde published his *Love Songs of Connacht* and married Lucy Kurtz, daughter of a German research chemist who had left Russia to settle in England. Those close to the family recall that Lucy Kurtz Hyde throughout their marriage had no interest in Hyde's Irish work, never learned a word of Irish herself, yet felt that his countrymen did not appreciate what Hyde had done for them. Her annoyance at the intrusion of the presidency of Ireland into their lives in 1938 was ill-concealed. She bore Hyde two daughters, Nuala, who died of consumption in 1916, and Una, who became the wife of James Sealy, a Dublin judge.

In 1896 Hyde sought appointment to the professorship of Irish at his alma mater, Trinity College, and was rejected after bitter opposition to his application led by Dr. Salmon, Trinity's Provost, and Robert Atkinson, Trinity's authority on Celtic studies, who apparently convinced Salmon that Hyde had only what Atkinson termed "Baboon Irish." Rising to Hyde's defense in this battle was Standish O'Grady, writing from London on 19 March 1896: "The perusal of these books should suffice to convince any honest and competent judge that their author or editor . . . must possess the Irish language practically and as a living tongue. . . . " O'Grady refutes the doubtings and questionings of Hyde's competence in Irish and concludes "As for Trinity College, in all Irish matters, it is a Leviathan in whose nose is a hook

whereby it is turned as one man listeth." Hyde's battle
with Trinity, "that English fort in Ireland" he called it,
continued for many years, and in his preface to *A
Literary History of Ireland* (1899) he vehemently attacked
the studied contempt for all things Irish that he had first
witnessed at Trinity during his student years.

Following the success of *Love Songs of Connacht,* which
Yeats would quickly acknowledge as "the coming of a
new power into literature," Hyde pushed his collecting
and recording as time allowed. His interest in the blind
poet Raftery brought him his first meeting with Yeats's
patroness, Lady Augusta Gregory, upon whom *Love
Songs* had made a considerable impact according to her
biographer. Their first meeting was at Edward Martyn's
"Tullira" in the summer of 1898 when Hyde appeared
with a bicycle broken while he had been searching the
neighborhood for those who had recollection of the blind
poet Raftery brought him his first meeting with Yeats's
Coole Park for a shooting party. Lady Gregory recalled
later that some of her neighbors, wives of the local Anglo-
Irish gentry, had sniffed that Hyde "cannot be a gentleman if he speaks Irish." But the gentleman who spoke Irish
and translated the *Love Songs* made a great hit with the
lady of Coole. In an undated letter to Hyde written from
Coole Park she reports on her visit to Spiddal: It was
"quite an Irish speaking place, and though I picked up
a few sea stories for Mr. Yeats and even, when he came
there, was able to introduce him to a fairy doctor, it
was a great drawback not knowing the language."
She had also tried to interest two Irish-speaking schoolmasters in collecting stories for Hyde: "I could hear
the people singing Irish songs as we passed the houses,

and in a house Mr. Yeats and I went to we heard some, and had them translated, modern songs and very charming about three young men who had been drowned off Aran, and about a young man who had been lured from the girls of his village by a girl from Galway, and how they flouted him afterwards.''

In the Christmas season of 1898, on Lady Gregory's invitation, Hyde produced a Punch and Judy show in Irish for the school feast at Coole. Assisted by Miss Borthwick, his associate in Irish language teaching, he triumphed in scenes where he scolded the baby in Gaelic, for many of his young audience had heard the same words used in their scoldings at home. According to her biographer, Lady Gregory saw this Christmas production as the beginning of modern Irish drama. In January, 1899, the Kiltartan branch of the Gaelic League was formed, and Hyde had found another influential and willing collaborator in the language cause.

Hyde was convinced that the Gaelic League could foster the spread of Irish through the production of plays written in the vernacular, and in the following summer he and Yeats worked at Coole on the scenario of *Casadh an tSugan (The Twisting of the Rope)*, based on a tale that Hyde had first published in 1893 in *Love Songs of Connacht*. (It had appeared there under the title ''The Soosheen Bawn''.) After much writing and rewriting, *The Twisting of the Rope* was presented at the Gaiety Theatre in Dublin on 21 October 1901 with a cast composed of members of the Gaelic League Amateur Dramatic Society. Hyde played the principal part with vigor: eyes gleaming and walrus mustaches rampant in the love-making scenes. The reception given this, the first Gaelic play produced in any theater, spurred Hyde to develop more such plays with the help of Yeats and Lady Gregory. Looking back on their times together at Coole, Yeats wrote his impressions of Hyde's working habits in the *Autobiography:* "He had the folk mind as no modern man has had it, its qualities and its defects. . . . he wrote all day, whether in verse or prose, and without apparent effort. Effort was there, but in the unconscious. . . . He wrote in joy and at great speed because emotion brought the appropriate word. Nothing in that language of his was abstract, nothing worn-out; he need not, as must the writer of some language exhausted by modern civilisation, reject word after word, cadence after cadence; he had escaped our perpetual, painful, purification."

Among the plays written by Hyde in Irish both to help the language movement and provide material for the amateur actors in the League were *The Lost Saint,* written on a legend provided by Yeats, and *The Nativity Play,* done on a scenario that Lady Gregory and Yeats had prepared for Hyde. The latter eventually was produced at the Abbey Theatre in an English translation by Lady Gregory on 5 January 1911. Close collaboration between Hyde and Lady Gregory brought forth *The Marriage,* first given at the Galway *feis* of 1902. Hyde played the part of Blind Raftery in this adaptation of a tale told Lady Gregory about how Raftery came to a poor cottage where two young people were to be married and how by his gift of song and laughter "had made a feast where no feast was." Of Hyde's performance Lady Gregory noted: "It will be hard to forget the blind poet, as he was represented on the stage by the living poet so full of kindly humor, of humorous malice, of dignity under his poor clothing, or the wistful ghostly sigh with which he went out the door at the end." The collaboration of the vicar's son from Roscommon with the lady of the Big House produced also *The Poorhouse*, later to be rewritten by Lady Gregory and given its new title *The Workhouse Ward*. Her account of their joint effort is given in Lady Gregory's *Our Irish Theatre:* "As to *The Poorhouse*, the idea came from a visit to Gort Workhouse one day . . . I intended to write the full dialogues myself, but Mr. Yeats thought a new Gaelic play more useful for the moment, and rather sadly I laid that part of the work upon Dr. Hyde. It was all for the best in the end, for the little play, when we put it on at the Abbey [3 April 1907] did not go very well. It seemed to ravel out into loose ends, and we did not repeat it; nor did the Gaelic players like it as well as *The Marriage* and *The Lost Saint*. . . . " The second version, *The Workhouse Ward,* produced at the Abbey on 20 April 1908, was completely recast by Lady Gregory with only three essential characters—two old men and the sister—and a completely new dialogue.

In tribute to Hyde's part in the success of the Abbey Theatre, Lady Gregory wrote in 1911: ". . . we are always grateful to him for that *Twisting of the Rope* in which he played with so much gaiety, ease and charm. But in founding the Gaelic League, he had done far more than that for our work. It was a movement for keeping the Irish language a spoken one, with, as a chief end, the preserving of our own nationality. That does not sound like the beginning of a revolution, yet it was one. It was the discovery, the disclosure of the folk-learning, the folk-poetry, the folk-tradition. . . . All our writers, Mr.

Yeats himself, were influenced by it. Mr. Synge found what he had lacked before—fable, emotion, style."

In the audience at one of the Gaiety productions of *Casadh an tSugan* in October 1901 was John Millington Synge who, his biographers report, was "most struck by the Gaelic play in which Hyde himself had acted." Five years later, Synge wrote of *Casadh an tSugan* that he thought it important "because it gave a new direction and impulse to Irish drama." In reviewing Lady Gregory's *Cuchullain of Muirthemne* in June 1902, Synge complimented her on her handling of the Anglo-Irish dialect of Kiltartan, but took issue with Yeats's claim in the introduction to the book that she had been the first to use it. Rather, said Synge, the credit should go to Douglas Hyde who had "used a very similar language in his translations of the *Love Songs of Connacht.*"

Another important convert to Hyde's crusade to save the Irish language was the novelist George Moore. In an undated letter probably written to Hyde from London shortly before his move to 4 Upper Ely Place in Dublin in 1901, Moore heaped praise on Hyde's Irish poems that he had read in Lady Gregory's translations:

". . . and [I] wish I could find words to express my admiration for them. They are as good as Villon and Heine and will be read always as Horace is read by scholars if the language dies, if we do not succeed in saving the language. The extraordinary merit of your poems you owe in a great measure to the language you are writing in. . . a language as young as English was in Shakespearean days. *Speak Irish, write Irish, think Irish.* . . . Ah my dear friend you were born to do a certain work and when a man is born to do a thing it gets done."

Upon his arrival in Dublin, Moore became increasingly caught up in the excitement of the Gaelic League and the move to establish a national theater. While his enthusiasm lasted, Moore was of great help to the movement, even making a painstaking effort to help Hyde improve his play *The Tinker and the Fairy*. In seven letters held by the National Library of Ireland and written in the spring of 1902 Moore offered advice for strengthening the play. On March 24 he wrote Hyde: ". . . I am not quite sure that some more philosophical statements might not be introduced into the tinker's soliloquy at the end of the play. He is no longer a tinker, he is abstract humanity, and you can make him say what you like regardless of individual limitations."

Moore not only criticized the tinker's soliloquy in the play and questioned Hyde as to whether the meter should be preserved in the English version; he even experimented with the beat in one stanza.

Moore wrote on March 28: "I do not think that the addition you sent me this morning is an improvement. The play is perfect except for one or two little things— minute touches. I think for it to have a perfect literary form the dialogue might be lengthened a little bit here and there. In places where you put four words I think there might be seven or eight. . . ." On March 29 Moore wrote that he had read the play several times ". . . and am convinced that it is very well as it stands—from my point of view it is perfect." Revealing again his high dedication to his craft, Moore offered a final suggestion for improvement in a letter of April 2: "I do not think there is anything to correct except perhaps the fairy's first speech. . . . Just write a few words into it."

The Tinker and the Fairy was first produced in Moore's garden with (according to Moore) Kuno Meyer, the eminent Celticist, prompting Hyde's Irish occasionally. Published in 1902 with an English translation by Belinda Butler, it was performed at the Gaiety Theatre in Irish in 1903 with Hyde and Sinead Ni Fhlannagain (later Mrs. Eamon de Valera) in the principal parts. On 15 January 1912, it was produced in Irish at the Abbey Theatre.

Moore's involvement in the Gaelic League and his solid help in revising Hyde's play reflects well on both men: Hyde for attracting divergent, even eccentric personalities to his cause and Moore for firmly insisting on craftsman's standards in a play written chiefly for propaganda purposes.

By the dates of the writing of his fictional autobiography (*Hail and Farewell*, 1904–11), however, Moore's feelings toward Hyde and the League were anything but warm. In *Ave* (the first volume of *Hail and Farewell!*), Moore's appraisal of Hyde was condescending, unflattering, and meanly anthropological: "He had been sitting on my side of the table, and I could only catch glimpses of his profile between the courses when he looked up at the waiter and asked him for more champagne, and the sparkling wine and the great yellow skull sloping backwards had seemed a little incongruous . . . . when Hyde began to speak Irish an instinctive repulsion rose up in me. . . . Hyde, too, perhaps on account of the language, perhaps it was his appearance, inspired a certain repulsion in me, which, however, I did not attempt to quell. It looked so like a native Irish speaker; or was it?—and perhaps it was this—he looked like an imitation native Irish speaker; in other words, like a stage Irishman."

Yet if Moore came to mock the Gaelic League and Hyde's hopes for it, by 1905, the year of Hyde's trip to America to raise funds for the League, its influence had reached into every corner of Ireland. Activities varied from open-air excursions and outings, games and competitions in the country to amateur dramatic performances. Myles Dillon tells that in Ballaghadereen, but a few miles from Frenchpark, one of the leading citizens, after learning Irish, prevailed on the local amateur dramatic group to perform his Irish play in their repertory given at the Dublin Rotunda. Gaelic Leaguers began addressing parcels in Irish, and when the parcels and letters were turned back by the Post Office Hyde went to London, interviewed the postmaster general, and returned to announce that parcels addressed in Irish would be accepted. Intellectuals like Father Peter O'Leary and Eóin MacNeill joined the League and became vice-presidents. Protestants, Catholics, unionists, and nationalists were able for the first time to find a common ground in the language cause. When in 1901 his old foes at Trinity, Mahaffy and Atkinson, tried to keep Irish off the secondary school curriculum, Hyde turned to his scholar friends on the Continent to rally support for the study of Irish. Meanwhile, D. P. Moran, a Waterford native and London journalist, became a spokesman for the League's "buy Irish" campaign through his newspaper, the *Leader*. Among other causes Moran spoke out strongly against the Englishman's games of cricket and tennis in favor of traditional and authentic Irish games. Through its pressure, the League brought the closing of public houses on St. Patrick's day and the turning of that day into a national holiday. What Yeats had correctly called "a great popular movement" came into being in slightly over ten years under Hyde's leadership, with over five hundred branches organized on the eve of his departure for America.

Hyde's drive had brought a tremendous boost to Irish self-esteem and brought him to the attention of John Quinn, an Irish-American millionaire who, even before meeting Hyde, had ordered his portrait done by John Butler Yeats. Quinn had seen Hyde at the Killeeneen *feis* of 31 August 1903 marking the erection of a stone —sponsored by Lady Gregory—to honor the blind poet Raftery. On 19 July 1904, Quinn wrote Hyde from New York: "Yeats has no doubt told you of his trip here and how badly you are needed to organize the country on behalf of the League." He met Hyde again in October 1904 at a reception held at Coole and lunched with him in Dublin on October 20. His aim was to lay plans for a trip to America to promote both Hyde and his cause for whom his admiration was based on the fact that both were native Irish, nonclerical, nonpolitical, and intellectual.

Although Yeats had praised Hyde in his American tour, the older Irish societies in the country were suspicious of the Gaelic League and its founder, who was both a Protestant and an intellectual. Quinn campaigned to allay their suspicions by writing to influential friends such as the Jesuit, John Wynne, to whom he pointed out that although Hyde was not Catholic, he was the best Irishman that Quinn had

ever known, "Catholic or not." With consummate
organizing skill, Quinn set up appearances for Hyde
before Irish groups across the country and arranged
a supplementary series of college lectures for Hyde's
personal benefit. A choice of four lectures was offered:
"The Gaelic Movement," "The Last Three Centuries
of Irish Literature," "The Folktale in Ireland," or
"The Poetic Literature of Ireland."

Hyde arrived in New York on 15 November 1905 and
made his way to Cambridge where his first major talk
was given at Harvard on November 20. As he had done
for Yeats, Quinn arranged a meeting for Hyde with
President Theodore Roosevelt. Hyde was pleased with
his reception at the White House. On 27 November 1905
he wrote: "The President seemed to know as much
about Irish literature and the ideals of the Gaelic League,
as I did myself almost, and spoke incessantly about
Irish saga and Irish literature. I think he will make an
appeal to the Irish-Americans to found chairs of Irish
in the Universities here; I hope so." Writing again
on 15 January 1906, Hyde recalled that Roosevelt had
spoken "a great deal about Irish saga and the ancient
Irish epics, and drew a most interesting comparison
between them and the Norse saga. He struck me as
being a scholar of the very broadest sympathies."

On 9 January 1906, Hyde spoke to an audience of
eight hundred in Milwaukee, sharing the platform with
the governor of the state and the Catholic Bishop Messmer.
He lectured on Irish to about six hundred persons at the
University of Wisconsin at Madison and noted his
approval of President Van Hise's determination to
bring that University to all the people of the state.

Speeches in Omaha, Elmira, Scranton, Buffalo, Rochester, Hartford, Springfield, and Boston brought in large contributions. In Chicago his appearance raised over six thousand dollars for the League, and he did equally well in St. Louis, Sacramento, and Seattle. When he and his wife left for home in the middle of June 1906, Hyde had raised more than eleven thousand pounds for the League. He wrote to Quinn in July after his triumphant reception in Dublin: "The whole of O'Connell Street was packed from side to side, and from the Rotunda to below Nelson's Pillar, with one solid mass of people, and they all with one accord cheered for John Quinn, as well they might. I left nobody under doubt as to whom the American success was due."

In 1908 the National University of Ireland was established, and Hyde was appointed to the chair of modern Irish in Dublin in the following year, a post that he held until his retirement in 1932. In yet another battle he led the League's successful campaign to install Irish as a compulsory subject for matriculation in the University. Meanwhile the move within the Gaelic League toward extremism and physical force was gaining momentum, with a resulting turn from Hyde's way of moderation and conciliation. A spokesman for the Sinn Feiners was a young barrister, Padraic Pearse, who put the revolutionary viewpoint bluntly in "The Coming Revolution" (1913): "Whenever Dr. Hyde, at a meeting at which I have had a chance of speaking after him, has produced his dove of peace, I have always been careful to produce my sword; and to tantalise him by saying that the Gaelic League has brought into Ireland 'Not Peace but a Sword.'" The revolutionaries won the day in August 1915, and Hyde resigned his presidency of the Gaelic League. In 1916 his *Legends of Saints and Sinners* was printed. The Easter Rising swirled about him, but according to those who have seen his diary for that period he reports only what he saw and heard without an opinion being registered. At the family table in Dublin, no discussion of the Rising was permitted. Hyde's innermost feelings at the time were probably revealed in his letter to John Quinn on 12 October 1916 where he wrote that the "League had been steered on the rocks by fools" and that the general outlook in Ireland was "as black as can be." In that same year he endured the death of his daughter Nuala, from consumption, but was able to take some small comfort from the Celtic ceremonial of her burial in which she was carried to her grave in the Portahard Church graveyard near Frenchpark by twenty young Irish bachelors.

Writing to Quinn in December 1921, during the great debate on the treaty, he declared: ". . . we seem to have really hammered out a measure of real freedom. . . . So far as I can see, we have got almost everything we want under the new treaty. . . . I think we got the very most we could have got without war, and war is too awful to contemplate again."

Hyde's summers from June through mid-September were spent at "Ratra" near Frenchpark, close by his father's church at Portahard. In his youth Hyde had watched "Ratra" being built and had later rented it from the French family, and then had it presented to him as a gift by the Gaelic League on his return from America. On his retirement from teaching in 1932, at the age of seventy-two, he sold his Dublin home and lived at "Ratra" year-round until his call to the presidency of Ireland in 1938. The routine at "Ratra" was one of reading, transcribing, and translating tales; shooting the bogs for snipe, partridge, pheasant, and hares. There were frequent visits from old friends and young men and women seeking his endorsement for teaching and civil service posts. Occasionally during their holidays, young seminarians from Maynooth would visit. Time permitted work on plants and flowers surrounding "Ratra" and frequent visits to his sister, Mrs. Cambreth Kane, who lived in "Glebe House" close by—his father's former rectory. Strolls were interrupted by encounters with children whom he would encourage to speak a few words of Irish and chats with their fathers about crops. A trip to Castlerea meant a round of golf on the course laid out on the grounds of Clonalis House, the home of his friend O'Conor Don. A favorite diversion was the walk to Lough Gara of the 1883 dream allegory where he kept his fishing boat. For any who had not heard it before, Hyde would tell the story of how he had once fallen through the bog turf into a subterranean illicit distillery where the shocked operators had offered him a sample of poteen served in an eggshell, the only available container for their unexpected guest, and how he had accepted their gift of a bottle of the stuff and used whisps of bog grass to stopper the bottle. According to those closest to him in those years, the talk covered all subjects but one—politics. Invariably he would shift the conversation to crops or the "running" of spirits when the day's political disputes were introduced. Those who saw him almost daily in those years report also that his knowledge of saints, holy days, sites of ancient monasteries, and local folklore was encyclopedic, but that creed for its own sake was a subject alien, even abhorrent to him. As one countryman recalled recently: "Dr. Hyde was an ecumenicist long before we heard anything about ecumenicism and when it was just a strange word hidden away in the recesses of the dictionary . . . and in this he was fifty years ahead of his time."

Politics and religion, "the two fruitful springs of pain and cruelty and heart scalding all over this earth. Can you deny it?" This had been the affirmation and the question hurled at young Hyde by Mr. Nogod in the dream recollected by the young Trinity divinity student from Roscommon. Over half a century later Hyde's mind was clear of any doubt as to his answer.

The End of a Ship
Is Wreckage

One need scarcely do more than read between the
lines describing Castlerea in *Slater's Directory of Ireland*
for 1856 to sense the odds facing Douglas Hyde as he
set out to revive Gaelic Ireland through its language
and folklore. This central Connacht market town 112
miles north and west of Dublin where Hyde would be
baptized in 1860 was "Anglicised" in every sense of
that word by 1856. And what social and economic
"Anglicisation" had begun toward the obliteration of
all things Gaelic would be finished by its twin accomplices,
famine and fever. Described in 1856 as "whitewashed. . .
with a clean and lively aspect" Castlerea like most Irish
towns had undergone torment only a decade before.
In September 1846, O'Conor Don, descendant of once-
proud medieval Connacht kings, had written in urgency
to the Commissary-General pleading that food be sent
to Castlerea to forestall impending starvation for the
cottagers around him. The Government saw its chance
to dispose of broken Army biscuits held in storage since
1843, but there is no evidence that the biscuits ever
arrived in Castlerea. Seven miles from Castlcrea at
Frenchpark, where Hyde grew up between 1867 and

1880, the Fall of 1846 had seen Lord French, a landlord with over twenty thousand acres, hanged in effigy by desperate men opposite the front door to his mansion. By October 1846, seventy-five hundred people in County Roscommon were existing on one meal of boiled cabbage leaves every two days. For thirty thousand inhabitants living in 135 square miles surrounding Frenchpark there was not one hospital to harbor the victims of the fever that swept through the huts and cottages on the heels of the famine. Hyde's "O's and Mac's," the "last of the Milesians" died by the score in the Castlerea Workhouse. As they died they were slid along sloping floor boards through the notorious "Black Gable" into a grave-pit filled with lime.

Lost forever with the corpses in the grave-pits of the famine years in Connacht were the poems, tales, proverbs, prayers, and songs of Gaelic oral tradition. Those of the peasantry who had not been humiliated or humbled through "Anglicisation" now had their dwindling ranks decimated by the horrors of famine and fever. It is not that Hyde was later able to recover so much of oral tradition that is astonishing, but rather that he could find any remnant of it at all by 1880. The account of an eighty-year-old woman in Donegal serves well to describe also what had happened in central Connacht: "It didn't matter who was related to you, your friend was whoever would give you a bite to put in your mouth. Sport and pastimes disappeared. Poetry, music and dancing stopped. They lost and forgot them all and when the times improved in other respects, these things never returned as they had been. (*Mharbh an gorta achan rud*) The famine killed everything."

Hyde's first book of folk tales appeared in 1889.

Leabhar Sgealaigheachta offered twenty stories collected from country men and women in their sixties and seventies who had miraculously lived through 1846–47. Several tales in the volume were contributed by William Larminie and a national schoolmaster in Galway. Hyde had previously published his first poems in Irish in *The Shamrock* during 1879–80, in that weekly's column called "Our Gaelic Department." Some of his Irish poetry also had appeared in *The Dublin University Review*, edited by T. W. Rolleston and later, George Coffey, and published monthly from 1884 to 1887. One of Hyde's poems lamenting the disappearance of the Irish people from their land appeared in the August 1886 number with the title *Smaointe Bhroin* (sad thoughts).

In six "Notes" appended to the Gaelic texts of *Leabhar Sgealaigheachta* Hyde regretfully used English. since, as he worte: "Certain friends pointed out to me the advisability of adding some explanatory observations on the text, which should prove useful to any who may use this book to learn Irish." He used his first "Note" as a vehicle for striking back at those who asked "Why keep Irish alive?" The answer, said Hyde, is that first, if Irish dies, its literature will go into obscurity and it deserves better. English is the language of strangers, and Irish preserved means a literature kept alive that is rich in legends, poems, and proverbs. All this will be lost if English supplants Irish as the language of the people. If the language must die, however, it should be the decision of the Irish people, not the dictate of an alien and oppressive culture. And yet, wrote Hyde, the Irish have never been given the right to make this choice. The confiscations of 1648 and 1691 and the intense efforts

of the Anglo-Irish gentry to "stamp out both the language
and institutions of a nation" have robbed the people of
their right to choose. Hyde was particularly caustic
about the successors to the planters, "the brutalized,
sensual, unsympathetic gentry of the last century, the
racing, blustering, drunken squireens, who usurped
the places" of the O'Conors, O'Briens, O'Donnells,
and other families of the Gaelic aristocracy. He also
berated the National schoolteachers of his own time
who beat their students for talking Irish, and all the
English-speaking petty officialdom who conspired
to keep the Irish language from showing its capabilities.
He is quiet concerning the complicity of Irish parents
with the schoolmasters in stamping out the language.
His final exhortation to his readers: ". . . if we allow
one of the finest and richest languages in Europe. . .
to die without a struggle it will be an everlasting
disgrace and a blighting stigma upon our nationality."

In his second "Note" Hyde explained that rather than
give a pure text, or a transcription of the stories exactly
as heard, he had written the stories as told to him with
spelling unchanged, correcting only errors of grammar
and inflection and occasionally substituting "a word here
and there in place of some barbaric half-Anglicised
compound used by my narrator in the heat of story-
telling." He admitted that his book would have little
philological value "since I have neither adopted the case-
endings of the older language, nor yet given the
new exactly as I found it." He apologized for not sup-
plying a phonetic transcription of the tales on the
grounds that the seventeen Irish letters are inadequate
for that job and that he would have had to invent or adapt

a new phonetic alphabet for the purpose. He did praise William Larminie, from whose manuscripts of phonetically written stories he took two tales for *Leabhar Sgealaigheachta*. Larminie had written him twice in 1888 pleading for the institution of phonetic spelling if Irish were to be kept alive. Athough unwilling to attempt this himself Hyde recognized the value of the phonetic approach: "Whosoever succeeds in applying a sound system of phonetics to the fixing of the various dialectic pronunciations of Ireland, before they die, will have done something of national importance."

In his next important collection, *Beside the Fire* (1890), Hyde presented fifteen folk tales from the Gaelic, half of which had already appeared in *Leabhar Sgealaigheachta*. This time he provided facing pages of Irish and his own English translations. *Beside the Fire* is dedicated to "those truly cultured and unselfish men, the poet-scribes and hedge-schoolmasters of the last century and the beginning of this—men who may well be called the last of the Milesians. . . . " In a fifty-page Preface, Hyde took some of his predecessors to task for not knowing Irish, cooking up tales to make them more palatable for English readers, and not telling readers who gave them their stories or where. Among those negligent in these respects he included Crofton Croker, Kennedy, Lady Wilde, and the American, Jeremiah Curtin, who although the best of the lot "leaves us in complete darkness as to where and from whom and how he collected these stories." Nevertheless, said Hyde, Curtin "has approached the fountainhead more nearly than any other." Hyde took pains to provide "the *exact language* of my informants, together with their names and various localities."

In his Preface he discussed the likenesses and differences between Scottish Gaelic stories and their Irish counterparts, stating his belief that the incidents of each story were remembered, not the language, and that each rendition of the story reflected the storyteller's own skill and eloquence rather than his dependence on an earlier version.

Hyde told of one of his Roscommon informants, "old Shawn Cunningham," that he did not speak English until he was fifteen years old and that he had been taught Irish by a hedge schoolmaster who had forced him to learn Irish by memorizing Irish poems. His next schoolmaster, however, "tied a piece of stick round his neck, and when he came to school in the morning the schoolmaster used to inspect the piece of wood and pretend that it told him how often he had spoken Irish when at home. In some cases the schoolmasters made the parents put a notch in the stick every time the child failed to speak English. He was beaten then, and always beaten whenever he was heard speaking a word of Irish, even though at the time he could hardly speak a word of English. His son and daughter now speak Irish, though not fluently, his grandchildren do not even understand it. He had at one time, as he expressed it, 'the full of a sack of stories,' but he had forgotten them. His grandchildren stood by his knee while he told me one or two, but it was evident they did not understand a word. His son and daughter laughed at them as nonsense."

Offering a close translation for each of fifteen tales Hyde described how English and Gaelic are opposed to one another in spirit and idiom and how, consequently, he had found translation to be hard work. He pointed out that the English spoken by three-quarters of the Irish is influenced heavily by Gaelic idiom—translations from the Irish that was the language of the speaker's father, grandfather, or great-grandfather. Hyde believed that where Irish itself has died out, the idiom of Anglo-Irish speech lives in perpetuity and even increases. He explained that he had not always translated the Irish idioms literally. He did not translate, for example, the Irish for "he died" by "he got death" since this literal translation was not adopted into Anglo-Irish. He did translate the Irish *ghnidheadh se sin* by "he used to do that," which is an Anglo-Irish effort to make a consuetudinal tense missing in English. Hyde avoided the pluperfect since no such tense exists in Irish.

Frank O'Connor calls Hyde's attempt to use the idiom of Anglo-Irish speech in translations of folk stories a "radical innovation for a rather conventional man" and hints that either W. B. Yeats had suggested it to Hyde, or that it was "an accidental discovery of Hyde himself."

In the story of "The Tailor and the Three Beasts," Hyde found episodes that reminded him of Jack the Giant Killer, possibly from an English source. He took note of the tale's nonsense ending: "The tailor and his wife came home to Galway. They gave me paper stockings and shoes of thick milk. I lost them since." Twenty Slavonic folk tales employ this kind of nonsense ending.

His Connacht informant for the first three tales in *Beside the Fire* was John Cunningham of Roscommon County whom Hyde described as being between seventy and eighty years old in 1893 and illiterate. Cunningham's account of "Paudyeen O'Kelly and the Weasel" has its setting in the fairy world of the arch-king and queen of the fairy host of Connacht. Connacht's fairy team wins the hurling match on Moytura and Paudyeen is given a purse of gold by the fairy king. Other local legends told to Hyde by old countrymen who had survived the famine and fever include the "Court of Crinnawn," a tale about a ruin close to Ballaghadereen. In his note on that tale, Hyde wrote of a local prophecy about the various great houses in Roscommon, including Clonalis of the O'Conors and Dungar, seat of the Frenches, and the verse in the prophecy that declares "no roof shall rise on Crinnawn." In this highly dramatic tale, there emerges from smoke, lightning, and thunder a figure with only one eye in his head who says that he is Crinnawn, son of Balor of the Evil Eye. He pays off friars to keep his secret, and when priests threaten him, he takes the roofs off houses by blowing blasts out of each nostril. This fearful personage is related to the figure in the legendary battle between the Tuatha De Danaan and the Fomorians on the fields of Moytura close to Kilmactranny, Hyde's home for his first seven years.

In a tale called "Trunk-without-Head" Hyde picked out an utterance by one of the characters: "You are a valiant man, and it stood you upon to be so, or you would be dead" and noted that it means "It was well for yourself it was so." He added that "this old Elizabethan idiom is of frequent occurence in Connacht English, having with many other Elizabethanisms, either filtered its way across the island from the Pale, or else been picked up by the people from the English peasantry with whom they have to associate when they go over to England to reap the harvest."

The setting of another tale, "The Hags of the Long Teeth," is Loughlinn, a village four miles northwest of Castlerea. The story, which Hyde got from a story-teller in Ballinrobe, tells of a party of Dublin sports who come to Lough Glinn for hunting and fishing and meet more than they bargained for, including a giant black dog that catches their rifle balls in his mouth, chews them, and flings them to the ground. The Dublin sports also meet six sisters with long teeth and seven vultures in a tree all of whom are eventually banished by a bishop after he makes a secret agreement with the hag of the long tooth.

Hyde concluded *Beside the Fire* with extensive notes on the Irish text, glossing hard words and giving variant spellings and pronunciations for the same word in Connacht and other provinces. He also supplied an "Index of Incidents" for the convenience of the reader who is interested in comparing and contrasting his stories with others he has heard or read.

In *Love Songs of Connacht* (1893) Hyde tested his skill as a poet and translator on Gaelic folkverse that had escaped obliteration in the famine years. Before Hyde, there were translations from the Gaelic done in the eighteenth century, the first full volume being the work of Charlotte Brooke in 1788. There also had been numerous English versions of the old poetry printed before 1850. An interest in the harpers' airs had led to an interest in the words, and in 1831 James Hardiman had published *Irish Minstrelsy* in two parts: the first a group of poems by the harpist Carolan; the second called "Bacchanalian and Sentimental Songs." Both Samuel Ferguson and James Clarence Mangan had tried their hands at "Englishing" Gaelic verse, the latter alternating between literal and free translations. Edward Walsh and J. J. Callanan had printed transla-tions of Gaelic poems before 1850, and in 1860 George Sigerson had published his *Poets and Poetry of Munster,* an anthology of Irish songs with metrical translations.

In the Preface to *Love Songs of Connacht,* addressed to Sigerson, Hyde said that he offered the "Love-Songs of a single province merely, where I either took down in each county of Connacht from the lips of the Irish-speaking peasantry—a class which is disappearing with most alarming rapidity—or extracted from MSS. in my own possession, or from some lent to me, made by different scribes during this century. . . ." He had no regrets for having made literal translations since they should be useful to foreign philologists ignorant of Irish idiom and useful also to Hyde's contemporaries in Ireland who may have wished to learn the native language. He added that in some of his translations into English verse he had tried to reproduce the vowel-rhymes as well as the exact meters of the originals. Other poems translated into English prose were his efforts to reproduce literally the Irish originals. He admitted to having inserted "a few conjectural emendations of many passages and works which appeared unintelligible." He also was careful to point out that he had provided in his footnotes an honest reading of the original manuscripts using the words of the reciter no matter how corrupt they may have sounded.

Admitting that the Irish are capable of "loud-tongued, sporting, devil-may-care songs" as well as "truly gentle, smooth, fair loving poems" Hyde claimed that as an oppressed race, the Irish have been reduced to these opposites of foolish mirth and keening lamentation. He freely admitted that grief, melancholy, and trouble stamp his *Love Songs*. Many, he said, are by anonymous country women whose directness of expression reveals their capacity for love and simultaneously their frustration with custom, tradition, poverty, and the match-making game that often defeated them. Typical of such poems are these verses from "If I were to go West":

> If I were to go west, it is from the west I would not come,
> On the hill that was highest, 'tis on it I would stand,
> It is the fragrant branch I would soonest pluck,
> And it is my own love I would quickest follow.
>
> My heart is as black as a sloe,
> Or as a black coal that would be burnt in a forge,
> As the sole of a shoe upon white halls,
> And there is great melancholy over my laugh.
>
> . . . .
>
> Time it is for me to leave this town,
> The stone is sharp in it, and the mould is cold;
> It was in it I got a voice (blame), without riches
> And a heavy word from the band who back-bite.
>
> I denounce love; woe is she who gave it
> To the son of yon woman, who never undertood it.
> My heart in my middle, sure he has left it black,
> And I do not see him on the street or in any place.

From the lips of an old woman in Sligo Hyde heard "the Brow of the Red Mountain" but, he wrote, "it was mixed up and mingled with other bad verses, and for that reason I give part of it out of my manuscript and part that is not in the manuscript, as I got it from the old woman." The speaker laments that she is denied the love of her choice:

I am sitting up
Since the moon rose last night,
And putting down a fire,
And ever kindling it diligently;
The people of the house
Are lying down, and I by myself.
The cocks are crowing,
And the land is asleep but me.

That I may never leave the world
Till I loose from me the ill-luck,
Till I have cows and sheep
And my one desire of a boy.

I would not think the night long
That I would be stretched by his smooth white breast
And sure I would allow the race of Eve
After that to say their choice thing (*of me*).

From Biddy Crummy, living in her bog cabin near Frenchpark, Hyde took "Mo bhron ar an bhfairrge" ("My Grief on the Sea") the earliest version of which he had heard from a neighbor, Mrs. O'Rourke in September, 1877:

My grief on the sea,
How the waves of it roll!
For they heave between me
And the love of my soul!

Abandoned, forsaken,
To grief and to care,
Will the sea ever waken
Relief from despair?

. . . .

On a green bed of rushes

> All last night I lay,
> And I flung it abroad
> With the heat of the day.
>
> And my love came behind me—
> He came from the South;
> His breast to my bosom,
> His mouth to my mouth.

Not only did Hyde offer bilingual versions and literal translations of the folk-verses but he usually supplied a prose commentary on the poem in which he preserved the Gaelic idiom in English syntax. For example, this commentary accompanied "Ringleted Youth of My Love": "There is another melodious piece in which we find the same expression 'star of knowledge' and a lovely expression it is. It is making us understand it is, that there be's double knowledge and greatly increased sharp-sightedness to him who is in love. The love is like a star, and it is like a star of knowledge on account of the way in which it opens our senses so that we be double more light, more lively and more sharp than we were before. We understand then the glory and the beauty of the world in a way we never understood it until that." Following the prose commentary comes his own translation of the poem. I give one representative stanza here:

> Ringleted youth of my love,
> With thy locks loosely bound behind thee,
> You passed by the road above,
> But you never came in to find me;
> Where were the harm for you
> If you came for a little to see me,
> Your kiss is a wakening dew
> Were I ever so ill or so dreamy.

In a footnote Hyde then gave a literal translation for the poem: "O youth of the bound back hair, With whom I was once together You went by this way last night, And you did not come to see me. I thought no harm would be done you If you were to come and to ask for me, And sure it is your little kiss would give comfort, If I were in the midst of a fever."

In a review of the 1904 Dun Emer edition of *Love Songs of Connacht* with its preface by W. B. Yeats, the writer alluded to Hyde's "workmanlike translation . . . with a light and practised hand he gives, in fine English, a rendering that generally retains much of the elusive character of the original." The reviewer was also impressed by Hyde's skill in Englishing the originals without anglicizing them. Hyde had tried where others had failed. Possessed of a deep knowledge of Irish literature and folklore but a less-than-perfect command of the dialect, he responded to the finer points of sense, rhythm, and diction, and wherever he could not get an expression exactly correct in English, he would simply model the syntax on what he found in Gaelic.

Much taken with the Roscommon love story of Thomas Costello and Una MacDermott, Hyde gave ten pages of background material on the lovers and the version of the poem "Oona Waun" (Fair Una), which had come from his Roscommon informants Seamus O'Hart, Walter Sherlock, and Martin O'Brennan. "Strong Thomas" Costello was a legendary figure for his hero-feats: ". . . the old people in Counties Roscommon and Sligo used to have as many stories about him as would keep a person listening to them for an entire night, but I did not collect them all when I was able, and now I cannot find them." The story that Hyde had heard as a boy told of Una's separation from Thomas by her father, The MacDermott, and how a combination of events, including her lover's pride and hot temper, kept them apart. After her death, Costello is buried at his request in the same graveyard with Una on the same small island in Lough Key near Boyle.

Hyde's commentary on the poem ended: ". . . and there grew an ash-tree out of Una's grave and another tree out of the grave of Costello, and they inclined towards one another, and they did not cease from growing until the two tops were met and bent upon one another in the middle of the graveyard and people who saw them said they were that way still, but I was lately on the brink of Lough Cé and could not see them. I was not, however, on the island."

In "The Soosheen Bawn," part of which Hardiman had printed as "The Twisting of the Rope," Hyde found the makings for his *Casadh and tSugan,* eventually to be produced in Dublin as the first Irish play of modern times. He gave a summary of the poem in Gaelic and then in a faithful English translation: "'Tis the cause of this song—a bard who gave love to a young woman, and he came into the house where she herself was with her mother at the fall of night. The old woman was angry, him to come, and she thought to herself what would be the best way to put him out again, and she began twisting a suggaun, or straw rope. She held the straw, and she put the bard a-twisting it. The bard was going backwards according as the suggaun was a-lengthening, until at last he went out on the door and he ever twisting. . . . " *Casadh an tSugan* was produced at the Abbey Theatre as late as 1938, and Brendan Behan's *The Quare Fellow* began life as *The Twisting of Another Rope,* a one-act play with a wry play on Hyde's title.

The last poem in *Love Songs of Connacht* is "The Roman Earl," given, said Hyde, as "a counsel against women . . . by some morose old man, no doubt." He placed it here to counterbalance all that praise of women appearing in the earlier poems. Rather than a song heard in a bog cabin, however, it was taken from a manuscript in Hyde's possession written by John O'Donovan, "the greatest of Irish scholars."

He concluded by writing: "I have now done with the love songs. I shall give no other of them here. There is no sort of song amongst the peasantry more plentiful than they. . . . All that I have given up to this let them serve as examples of the way in which the Connacht peasant puts his love-thoughts into song and verse, whether it be hope or despair, grief or joy, that affect him."

Few of Hyde's translations from *Love Songs of Connacht* have been included in anthologies. *The Oxford Book of Irish Verse,* edited by Donagh MacDonagh and Lennox Robinson, contains five of the love-songs, although the "corrected" edition of 1959 still gives wrong birth and death dates for Hyde and he is ignored in the editors' Introduction to their collection. In his *Love Poems of the Irish* (1967), Seán Lucy prints eight of Hyde's translations of Gaelic folkverse, calling him "the best [translator] of his generation and one of the best of any." In *Poetry in Modern Ireland* (1951) Austin Clarke praises *Love Songs of Con-*

nacht for having revealed to young writers "an entire imaginative tradition" and for having "preserved the idiom of the Gaelic sentences not only in his literal prose versions of many of the poems, but also in the translation of his commentary." Synge's probable debt to Hyde was acknowledged early on by Padraic Colum, who saw the prose translations of the Connacht lyrics as offering a new medium that would emerge in the poetic dialogue of Synge's plays and the narrative of Lady Gregory's stories. For Daniel Corkery, Hyde's *Love Songs of Connacht* had taught Synge to strive in his style for "a directness and absence of the merely literary." Whether, as Lady Gregory's biographer has claimed, the Irish peasantry now saw Hyde as a reincarnation of their last great wandering poet, Blind Raftery, who had died sixty years earlier, is doubtful. What is true is that the *Love Songs of Connacht* were a strange and delightful discovery to a whole generation, and W. B. Yeats would concede that the uncommon rustic from Roscommon, Douglas Hyde, son of the Vicar of Frenchpark, had loosed "a new power into literature" from a beautiful but inhospitable world where "everything was so old that it was steeped in the heart. . . . "

In his *Three Sorrows of Story-Telling* (1895) Hyde included his own "Deirdre," which had captured the Vice-Chancellor's Prize for him at Trinity College in 1887. "Deirdre" along with the other two *Sorrows of Story-Telling*—"The Children of Lir" and "The Fate of the Children of Tuireann"—all appear here in undistinguished English iambics. To these Hyde added several ballads of St. Columcille in which he had either followed the Latin of Bishop Adamnan or had translated directly from the Irish. From what he described as "a dirty little black manuscript of my own" he made a translation of "The Children of Lir" that is approximately the same length as the original Gaelic version. His "Deirdre" is somewhat shortened over the original and the "Children of Tuireann" is much longer in its original form. He justified his cutting of the latter tale on grounds of preserving its epic unity. He follows his own English translations with three extracts in literal translation to show more clearly what they were like in the original. Always ready to draw on his intimate knowledge of Connacht legends, tales, and superstitions he wrote: "I know one man who had shot a swan, and his father would not allow it to be eaten"— he concluded that the swan superstition had a pagan origin. At another point he related how his old Connacht informants still used "Tuatha De Danaan" when alluding to "the invisible people of fairyland."

A Literary History of Ireland (1899) established Hyde firmly as a scholar, and the work is still a good if somewhat dated introduction to the subject. The book is dedicated to the Gaelic League whose presidency he had assumed at its founding in 1893: "To the members of the Gaelic League, the only body in Ireland which appears to realize the fact that Ireland has a past, has a history, has a literature, and the only body in Ireland which seeks to render the present a rational continuation of the past, I dedicate this attempt at a review of that literature which despite its present neglected position they feel and know to be a true possession of national importance."

Unquestionably a pioneer scholarly work, Hyde's *Literary History* also consistently reflects the deep impres-

sion registered in the mind of the boy growing up in
Sligo and Roscommon. Never are his illustrations and
examples far from home. Speculating, concerning the
etymology of *Gal* in *Galatian,* Hyde wrote: "This was actually a living word as recently as ten years ago. I knew an
old man who often used it in the sense of 'spirit,' 'fire,'
'energy.' He used to say *cuir gal ann*, meaning do it bravely,
energetically. This was in the County Roscommon. . . ."
He took note of the O'Conor Don ancestors, Turlogh,
third last high king, and Roderick, the last of all the high
kings of Ireland. Scattered through the *Literary History* are
allusions to the genealogy of this ancient Gaelic family
whose seat, Clonalis House in Castlerea, Hyde had visited on so many occasions. When he needed evidence to
support his skepticism for place-names as reliable cor-
roborators of myth, history, and tales he went to fabled
Queen Medb of Rathcroghan, close to his boyhood
home: "There is never a camping-ground of Meve's army
on their march a century B.C. from Rathcroghan in Roscommon to the plain of Mochruime in Louth, and
never a skirmish fought by them that has not given its
name to some plain, or camping-ground, or ford." For
illustration of the intermixture and crossing of the Gaelic aristocracy through centuries his best example is The
MacDermott of Moylurg, ancestor of The MacDermott
who was still called "Prince of Coolavin" in Hyde's day.
Anxious to demonstrate how the ear and memory
worked to preserve ancient poetry in Ireland he furnish-
ed an example nearest his boyhood home: "I have heard
from peasants stanzas composed by Donogha Mor
O'Daly of Boyle in the thirteenth century. . . . I have
again heard verses in which the measure and sense were
preserved, but found on comparing them with MSS, that

several obsolete words had been altered. . . . " In discussing the early sagas and romances, Hyde gave ample space to literary accounts of the two battles at Moytura, first between the Tuatha De Danaan and the Firbolg and then between the Tuatha De Danaan and the Fomorians. The legendary site of these battles was a short distance from Kilmactranny and Frenchpark, and when Hyde confessed that the mythological cycle had for him "a shadowy sense of vagueness, vastness, uncertainty" there was an echo of his boyhood association with the old countrymen who made Moytura vivid for their listeners. Even his speculations concerning the origin of the name of the River Shannon owe much to Hyde's collecting effort. He remembered one lengthy Roscommon poem of 1798 that had two different etymologies and names for the river in its several hundred verses and added that he had found a different version for the origin of the river in another folktale he had recently set down from a Roscommon native. Again, Hyde's Roscommon ties appeared when he told in the *Literary History* that he had been allowed to print some extracts from a good manuscript of Keating's "Three Shafts of Death" in the possession of O'Conor Don at Clonalis House. When he wrote of Mac Firbis, a contemporary of Keating, Hyde was reminded that this was the famous historian of Connacht who descended from Dathi, the last pagan monarch of Ireland whose supposed burial stone Hyde had seen at Rathcroghan. When he discussed the fates of manuscripts of Irish saints' lives Hyde told how he once sought a voluminous life of St. Attracta, a Roscommon saint, supposedly held by The MacDermott of Coolavin, only to find that it had been lent and lost.

As an objective job of literary scholarship, *A Literary*

History of Ireland comes off fairly well by present-day standards. Hyde was honest in admitting that pre-Patrician history in Ireland is dependent on accounts given in twelfth-and thirteenth-century manuscripts and that the early history of Ireland is "a mass of pseudo-historic narrative and myth, woven together into an apparently homogenous whole, and all now posing as real history." He was properly guarded in his estimate of any pre-Christian Irish pantheon, suggesting that although it may have been as highly organized as the Scandinavian, Ireland's early and complete conversion to Christianity had meant that only traces of its pagan deities remain. He admitted quickly that Irish genealogies that purport to go back to Adam "must be untrue inventions . . . we grant it." But he also argued that whereas Irish history prior to 300 B.C. is uncertain, the four great race stems converge within reach of the historical period— most importantly, the Eremon stem, which converges in Niall of the Nine Hostages, who came to the throne in 356, and Cairbre of the Liffey, who became High King in 267. He warned that for all their unreliability, the genealogical books *were* kept from the earliest introduction of the art of writing and probably kept with greater accuracy than any other records of the past. He was conservative in assessing the role of the Druids on the grounds that proof is lacking for some of their practices. In a chapter entitled "The Irish Elysium and Belief in Rebirth" he revealed that of sixty folk tales that he had collected "from the lips of the peasantry," roughly five contained allusions to a belief in another world full of life under the water and perhaps four spoke of a life inside the hills. He declared that early

Irish skill in metal and jewel-working, gold ornaments, and objects of clay and bronze argues for their seizing on the invention of writing and keeping their annals and genealogies all the more accurately because of the advanced state of their culture. He did a workmanlike job of the puzzle of the three Patricks and the poems and literature ascribed to that saint, although he seemed more comfortable with Columcille, a saint whose historicity is unquestioned and whose own poems Hyde could translate. He surveyed the monastic schools of the sixth and seventh centuries adequately for his time. Looking at the pagan elements in early Irish litarature, he called on foreign scholars' opinions to reinforce his belief that the Irish poems and sagas offer a genuine picture of pagan life in Europe "such as we look for in vain elsewhere." He placed great faith in the long Celtic memory as it worked to preserve early tales and legends. The Heroic or Red Branch Cycle to Hyde seemed to deal with the very history of the Milesians, the present Irish race; he wrote, "for the first time we seem at least to find ourselves on historic ground." In a twenty-page chapter on the *Táin* Hyde complained that there is a "great deal of verbiage and piling up [of] rather barren names" but granted that the epic has some well-conceived and well-executed incidents. Altogether Hyde devoted nearly seventy pages to the Red Branch material.

As with his translation of the *Táin*, Hyde worked from his own manuscript to provide a translation of the Finn episodes. The poetry that he knew best from collecting folk-verse from the seventeenth and eighteenth centuries came in for his highest praise: " . . . a wonderful arrangement of vowel sounds, so placed that in every accented syllable, first one vowel and then another fell upon the ear in all possible kinds of harmonious modifications." Dismayed with his own century, he did admit that in its early years when Irish was still generally spoken there were noble efforts by the people to preserve manuscripts by copying and recopying them and even sporadic production of poetry of "no very high order." For Hyde, the famine meant the utter collapse of the literary life of Ireland: "everything went by the board, thousands of manuscripts were lost. . . . "

In his introduction to the 1967 edition of *A Literary History,* Brian O'Cúiv calls Hyde no expert philologist. But despite his occasional errors of omission, inconsistencies, slips in dating manuscripts, and questionable views on some historical and literary matters Hyde was that rare scholar who was also deeply responsive to people and the more human aspects of the study of literature.

Hyde repeatedly reminded readers of the *Literary History* of the shattering blows struck against native Irish letters by the English beginning with the invasion of 1169: "that permanent war . . . which almost from its very commencement, *thoroughly arrested Irish development and disintegrated Irish life.*" His case for the steady destruction of all things Irish ranged from indictments of the Ordnance Survey for "Englishing" Irish place names of historic significance to laughing contempt for Trinity's ignorance of all things Irish. He related that when the subject of the Vice-Chancellor's prize in English verse was announced to be "Deirdre" it was found "that the students did not know what the word meant, or what Deirdre was, whether animal, vegetable, or mineral." Looking at his own time and particularly the scene in his native Connacht, Hyde blamed the loss of the language on the apathy of clergy who preached in English, the dislike of the Anglo-Irish gentry for spoken Irish, and the efforts of the National Board of Education to extirpate the national language. His final lament was for the rotting manuscripts that neither children nor adults had respect for, since they were written in a language worth nothing in their society.

Hyde's *Ubhla De'n Craoibh (Apples from the Branch)* is a collection of thirty-three of his own poems in Irish that had appeared in weekly newspapers. In the Preface to his Irish poems Hyde had written: "I would like better to make even one good verse in the language in which I am now writing, than to make a whole book of verse in English. For if there should any good be found in my English verses, it would not go to the credit of my mother Ireland, but of my stepmother, England." Of thirty-three poems in *Ubhla De'n Craoibh* several were odes written for Gaelic League occasions and others were ballads dealing with emigration, exile, defeat, and death. Several of Hyde's personal poems in *Ubhla De'n Craoibh* appealed deeply to Lady Gregory, and in her *Poets and Dreamers* (1903) she printed her translations of some, the first of which she believed had "as distinctive a quality as that of Villon or Heine":

> There are three fine devils eating my heart—
> They left me, my grief! without a thing:
> Sickness wrought, and Love wrought,
> And an empty pocket, my ruin and my woe.
> Poverty left me without a shirt,
> Barefooted, barelegged, without any covering;
> Sickness left me with my head weak

And my body miserable, an ugly thing.
Love left me like a coal upon the floor,
Like a half-burned sod, that is never put out,
Worse than the cough, worse than the fever itself,
Worse than any curse at all under the sun,
Worse than the great poverty
Is the devil that is called "Love" by the people.
And if I were in my young youth again,
I would not take, or give, or ask for a kiss!

Apologetic for her bare prose translations, saying that even if they give the heart of a poem "too much is lost in losing the outward likeness," Lady Gregory nevertheless did justice to these stanzas from Hyde's prophetic poem, "There is a Change Coming":

When that time comes it will come heavily;
He will grow fat that was lean;
He will grow lean that was fat,
Without shelter for the head, without mirth, without help.

The low will be raised up, says the poet;
The thing that was high will be thrown down again;
The world will be changed from end to end;
When that time comes it will come heavily.

If you yourself see this thing coming,
And the country without luck, without law, without authority,
Swept with the storm, without knowledge, without strength,
Remember my words, and don't let your heart break.

In *Religious Songs of Connacht* (1906) Hyde printed in two volumes close to 250 poems, stories, prayers, ranns, charms, blessings, and curses that he had begun collecting twenty years earlier. He assured his readers that over seventy-five of these were "taken down exactly as they came from the mouths of the people." All versions are put before the reader "exactly as I got them myself." His justification for presenting them was that religious songs disappear faster than other poems and simply cannot survive wherever English is substituted for the native Irish language.

Hyde noted the absence of anti-Protestant songs among the Catholic Irish as evidence of their tolerance even for those who would destroy their faith; swiped at the notorious Miler Macgrath who switched from Catholicism to Protestantism; looked closely at Donagh O'Daly, his first religious poet who was an early abbot of Boyle Abbey before his death in 1244. He gave O'Daly's "My Son Remember," one of many that he had heard recited by the old people of Roscommon. He offered examples of Marian poetry and printed the "Dialogue Between the Priest and the Poor Man"—a satire of a priest whom the poet thought cared too much for the things of this world. As a specimen of the many poems dealing with the quarrels of Ossian and St. Patrick, Hyde printed "Oscar of the Flail" which he had heard from his Roscommon friend, John Cunningham. Another sample of the Fenian-Patrick controversy comes in the poem entitled "Ossian in Elphin," versions of which he had heard in Roscommon cabins. As he had done in *Love Songs of Connacht*, Hyde supplied the Irish text for each poem, a free translation of the poem, and a literal prose translation at the bottom of each. His "Ossian in Elphin" came from a Belfast manuscript that corroborated Elphin as the first meeting place of the famous saint and the saga hero:

Long was last night in cold Elphin,
More long is tonight on its weary way,
Though yesterday seemed to me long and ill,
Yet longer still was this dreary day.

And, long for me, is each hour new-born,
Lost and forlorn with grinding grief
For the hunting lands, and the Fenian bands,
And the long-haired generous Fenian Chief.

. . . .

Would I were gone from this evil earth,
I am wan with dearth, I am old and thin,
Carrying stones in my own despite,
—Long is to-night in cold Elphin.

Ask O Patrick of God, for grace,
And tell me the place he will place me in
Or save my soul from the Ill One's might
—For long is to-night in cold Elphin.

Hyde's explanation for the Ossian-Patrick poems that he had collected is that they owe their composition to the people's need to save their beloved Fenians from the perdition prophesied for them by the clergy.

From the surviving range of religious poems he had come upon in Sligo, Roscommon, Mayo, and Galway, Hyde included a rousing war poem done by Blind Raftery in 1834 to encourage the peasantry fighting the Tithe War. In "The Poem of Tor," found in Mayo, he offered an example of the debate poems so popular in the Middle Ages. He included several samples of beggars' songs that predicted good things for the givers of alms. From a blind piper in Roscommon came a moving lyric, "If I were in Heaven." Then came a version of the Ten Commandments familiar, said Hyde, to everyone who spoke Irish in Connacht.

Another piece known to almost every old person in Connacht is a *Marainn,* possibly a dirge of Patrick. "I have often heard it, but it is very little of it I understood" he admitted. He believed it similar to the *Amra* of Columcille: "No two people seem to repeat it exactly alike, and a great part of it is always unintelligible. This and other poems like it have survived in oral tradition because of the promise with which they conclude: 'whoever will repeat them shall find heaven or some other blessing.'"

All of these poems, including those celebrating the Virgin, the Cross, Sunday, or the altar, are essential to "anyone who may desire to understand the soul of Connacht," according to Hyde.

In the second volume of *Religious Songs* Hyde presented more evidence of the variety of devotional poetry in Connacht. He offered a "Morning Prayer" from Connemara which he had also heard in Roscommon:

> The will of God be done by us,
> The law of God by kept by us,
> Our evil will controlled by us,
> Our tongue in check be held by us,
> Christ's passion understood by us,
> Each sinful crime be shunned by us,
> Much on the End be mused by us,
> And Death be blessed found by us.

. . . .

From one of his richest sources, Biddy Crummy in

the parish of Tibohine, Roscommon, Hyde got a verse "to be said when one is awakened by the chirping of the birds in the morning:

> A fragrant prayer upon the air
> My child taught me,
> Awaken there, the morn is fair,
> The birds sing free.
> Now dawns the day, awake and pray
> And bend the knee,
> The Lamb who lay beneath the clay
> Was slain for thee.

Observing the similarity of lines in many religious poems in Ireland and Gaelic Scotland, Hyde speculated that this was a result of the Church's practice of composing religious songs and hymns to instruct the people and teach them Christianity and that he had, in fact, collected the remains of such venerable poems. Common to Ireland and England are poems to say when "sparing" or "saving" the fire before retiring; that is covering a hot coal or ember so that it will provide ignition for the morning's fire. He printed several.

He singled out a prayer to say when going on a journey that had been heard on Aran mainly because he saw elements of the pre-Christian in it:

> Seven prayers, seven times over told,
> Mary left to her Son of old,
> Bride left to her mantle's length,
> God left to His own great strength.
> Between us and the Fairy Kind,
> Us and the People of the Wind,
> Us and the Water's drowning power,
>
> . . . .

Hyde noted the strong similarity between the Irish charms against toothache and trembling with their counterparts in Old English. He gave a charm for stopping blood collected in County Mayo and compared it to the Old English charm with Irish words embedded in it that is found in the Old English Bald's *Leech Book* composed in the tenth century.

At the end of volume two, in a poem entitled "The First of a Ship," Hyde heard resounding a note struck in his earliest days of collecting:

> The first of a ship—wood sheeting,
> The first of a kiln—stone-heaping,
> The first of a feast—good greeting,
> The first of good health—sound sleeping.
>
> The end of a ship—deep drowning,
> The end of kiln—red burning,
> The end of a feast—black frowning,
> The end of good health—white mourning.

He wrote: "The end! the end! The Gaels never forget it. *Respice finem,* 'Look to the end.' This is a word which used constantly to be in their mouths." And he concluded the *Religious Songs* with a rann that he often had heard in Connacht: "The little shaven gray scaldcrow shall go, the lark most beautiful upon a mountain shall go, the old man and his fame after him shall go, all who are alive and who ever came shall go."

In 1916, Hyde took refuge from the violence he himself had prophesied in his Irish poem "There is a Change Coming." In that year of revolt he printed yet another collection of folk tales, *Legends of Saints and*

Sinners, comprising mainly pieces with roots in Ireland's medieval Christian substratum. All of the forty-six items in *Saints and Sinners* owe their lives to the early Christianizing of the country. Some have Continental roots; others are of native invention. Many deal with episodes in the lives of Saints Patrick, Columcille, Moling, and Ciaran. Others are built around the figures of St. Peter and St. Paul. In his twenty-five years of collecting, wrote Hyde, he could count but one in four or five tales that was based in whole or in part on Christian conceptions and it is these that he presented in *Legends of Saints and Sinners.*

In "Oscar of the Flail" he gave a tale illustrating the tradition of confrontation between the last great Irish saga hero and the first Irish Christian hero—St. Patrick. He had taken it from John Cunningham, his early Roscommon hunting, fishing, Irish-speaking, story-telling mentor. "How Covetousness Came into the Church" caught Hyde's fancy and he turned it into rhyme as an example of the semicomic medieval morality. From a Middle Irish text he took "The Adventures of Leithin" and followed it with a folk version of the story that had St. Ciaran and two of his clerics added to it to make it more acceptable to monastic audiences.

His most interesting and significant retrievals from the detritus of monastic Ireland are tales derived from New Testament Apocrypha texts that circulated despite numerous prohibitions against reading them issued by the Roman Church. "The Burial of Jesus" collected in Galway seems to have come from the Apocryphal *Gospel of Nicodemus.* "St. Paul's Vision; or, The

Last End of the Man Who Lives a Bad Life" is an early Irish adaptation of the medieval *Visio Sancti Pauli*. Hyde found his version in a manuscript discarded in a loft of a farmhouse in Meath and estimated its age at about two hundred years. He offered an English translation from the Irish, in turn translated, he believed, from a now-lost Greek or Latin original. He related "The Last End" to two other medieval Irish popular tales employing material from the Apocrypha, *The Evernew Tongue* and *The Vision of Tundal*.

His finest effort as a collector and translator of folk tales and verse behind him, Hyde now turned to a more typical philological task—the editing of *The Conquests of Charlemagne* from the *Book of Lismore* and three other early vellum manuscripts. He offered it as an example of a number of pieces of medieval vernacular literature translated into late Middle or Early Modern Irish in the fourteenth and fifteenth centuries. The version in the *Book of Lismore* was taken from a Latin original, but Hyde related that other such chronicles were translated from French and Middle English. He believed his Lismore text was written in or about 1400 and traced the history of the Charlemagne story, mentioning five translations of it made into Old French at the beginning of the thirteenth century and a Welsh translation made no later than 1275. His careful edition of Charlemagne was prepared for the Irish Texts Society in 1917, an organization of which Hyde was the first president and whose first volume he had edited in 1901.

The next year appeared his *Catalogue of the Books and Manuscripts Comprising the Library of the Late Sir John T. Gilbert* in collaboration with D. J. O'Donoghue. Gilbert, who had died in 1898, was an antiquarian who had published a history of Dublin in 1861, in 1863 had attacked an incompetent edition of the public papers of Ireland, and had served as Librarian of the Royal Irish Academy for thirty-four years. The *Catalogue,* running to nearly one thousand pages, was a job that Hyde enjoyed judging by his introduction: ". . . this library is astonishingly rich in the materials of Irish history. There is matter here for a hundred valuable works on special periods and famous men connected with Ireland." Hyde was struck by the literary activity of Dublin from 1730 to 1800 reflected by the names of hundreds of printers, many of them doing beautiful work. He was equally impressed by the number of volumes printed on the Continent that showed an interest in Ireland and its people in the sixteenth, seventeenth, and eighteenth centuries. Among the more notable books he cataloged were a 1664 Spanish volume on St. Patrick's Purgatory; an Italian account of the same printed in 1660, and an Italian life of St. Patrick published in 1668. He also found and recorded an Italian life of St. Brigid (1676), another life of her in High German, and a history of Irish monasteries published in France in 1690. He was particularly touched by the number of books in Gilbert's library written by exiled Irishmen following Elizabeth's reign, Cromwell's Wars, and the Battle of the Boyne. Coming upon a copy of Sir John Davies's *Reports of Irish Law Cases* (1615), Hyde was shocked: "There is no possibility of fining down or explaining away the naked facts as his law cases show them, that an Irishman was *ipso facto* deprived of all legal rights and a lawful victim to every Englishman who desired to prey upon him." He noted with regret the negligible number of manuscripts in Irish in Gilbert's collection and the implications that this had for the fate of Irish manuscripts brought to the Royal Academy for purchase and then turned away by a librarian only slightly acquainted with Irish.

His triumphant American tour of 1905–6 was described by Hyde in *Mo Turus go hAmerice* (1937). His last major publication appeared in 1939. In it he returned to the folktales that had been his great source of inspiration in Roscommon during the first twenty years of his life. *Mayo Stories Told by Thomas Casey* (1939) is dedicated to the memory of Eleanor Hull and contains fourteen stories from the mouth of Thomas Casey, Kiltimagh, County Mayo. Casey could neither read nor write Irish, but ironically could write English fairly well. His stories had come from his grandfather, Shawn Bwee (Yellow John) O'Reilly, born near Castlebar in County Mayo. Casey considered himself a poet and once had told Hyde that his "grandest poem and the best I ever composed" was "in praise of you, your wife, and the house of Ratra." Unfortunately Hyde never transcribed it, being too immersed in capturing forever Casey's stories before the old man died. Casey, tinker by trade dealing in tinwares and mules, had also served a short time as a bailiff on a river near Kiltimagh, charged with putting a stop to the poaching of salmon. The last tale in Hyde's volume— "O'Casey Amongst the Fairies"—begins with an account of a horse-buying trip to the fair at Dunmore made by Casey on New Year's Day, 1900.

Casey's Irish was very close to the language that

Hyde had heard when he was young in the County Roscommon: "a little broken and corrupted" with eclipses and aspiration often left out and with grammar very bad in places. Nevertheless, writes Hyde, "I left it (and everything else) exactly as it was ... I was myself born and raised about two score miles to the east of Coillte-Mághach (Kilmitagh) and [he] speaks the same language, very nearly, that I heard round me when I was young."

Sensitive to the end of his life to the hardship and grinding poverty of the Irish peasantry, Hyde gave two stories by Casey that have in them grim details of the behind-the-scenes life of the peasant. *An Geirrfhiadh Sidhe,* the story of an indestructible fairy hare, shows the cruel aspects of the hunt and the kill and the butchering of small game. *An Bradan* describes the poaching of the salmon on the rivers even by those hired to guard against poachers.

As a youth Douglas Hyde had met the national memory in the cabins of Roscommon. Then ironically, as a scholar trained in an Ascendancy college, he retrieved and revived that memory and made its language an instrument to fashion a popular movement that would eventually help Ireland shake free of an alien grip. An Ascendancy child who early rejected the Ascendancy attitudes ticked off by Daniel Corkery—insolence, recklessness, cynicism, hardness—Hyde also rejected the Ascendancy role assigned him—that of a ·Protestant clergyman—as his unpublished allegory of 1883 reveals. But historians allude to him today as "the gentle Hyde" angry at not a living soul; a man of gentle demeanor, derived, they claim from his upbringing in an Irish-Anglican rectory. It is hard to find Hyde the poteen-drinker, snuff-user, crowd-mover. Rather is he depicted as the genteel idealist who thought that Ireland's twin traditions of poverty and spirituality should be made to find new expression in a fast-fading language for some ill-defined purpose.

There is no such ambiguity surrounding the literary Hyde. In his most important books, *Beside the Fire* (1890), *Love Songs of Connacht* (1893), and *Religious Songs of Connacht* (1906), he showed himself to be the most serious collector and translator of Gaelic verse. Yeats called the *Love Songs of Connacht* "one of those rare books in which art and life are one . . . completely blended." What had happened was that Hyde, the Ascendancy man, himself sprung free of that class's worst attributes, had created an Anglo-Irish speech that was a new literary idiom—a source for the rise of a new national drama in the hands of Synge and Lady Gregory. Its power and flexibility would also improve Hyde's own verse in Irish. With the ear and technical skill of a poet he would reproduce internal rimes and assonances and even the stresses of his Gaelic original. Ironically, his connection with the Ascendancy helped give prestige to the peasant dialect he had first uncovered as a folklorist and then revived as translator and poet.

His achievement is exemplified in his poem on Raftery —a triumph so complete that no one today knows with certainty whether it is the work of the blind Galway poet, or the Protestant rector's son from Roscommon:

> I am Raftery the poet,
> Full of hope and love,

With eyes that have no light,
With gentleness that has no misery.

Going west upon my pilgrimage
By the light of my heart,
Feeble and tired,
To the end of my road.

Behold me now,
And my face to a wall,
A-playing music,
Unto empty pockets.

Selected Bibliography

I. Primary Sources

Leabhar Sgealaigheachta. Dublin: 1889.

Beside the Fire. London: 1890.

"The Necessity for De-Anglicising Ireland." *The Revival of Irish Literature.* London: 1894, pp. 115–61.

Love Songs of Connacht. London and Dublin: 1893. Reprinted 1969, 1971.

The Three Sorrows of Story Telling. London: 1895.

The Story of Early Gaelic Literature. London: 1895.

A Literary History of Ireland. London: 1899; new ed. with introduction by Brian O'Cuiv. London and New York: 1967.

Four Irish Plays by Hyde, *The Twisting of the Rope, The Marriage, The Lost Saint,* and *The Nativity* are printed and translated by Lady Gregory in her *Poets and Dreamers.* Dublin: 1903. Reissued in 1967.

The Tinker and the Fairy. Dublin: 1902. Translated by Belinda Butler.

Songs Ascribed to Raftery. Dublin: 1903. Reprinted 1973.

Religious Songs of Connacht, 2 vols. London and Dublin:1906. Reprinted 1972 in one volume.

Legends of Saints and Sinners. Dublin: 1916.

The Conquests of Charlemagne, Irish Texts Society, vol. 19. London: 1917.

Catalogue of the Books and Manuscripts Comprising the Library of the Late Sir John T. Gilbert. Dublin: 1918. Compiled with D. O'Donoghue.

Mo Turus go hAmerice. Dublin: 1937.

Mayo Stories Told by Thomas Casey, Irish Texts Society, vol. 36. London: 1939.

II. Secondary Sources

Coffey, Diarmid. *Douglas Hyde*. Dublin: 1938.

Conner, Lester. "The Importance of Douglas Hyde to the Irish Literary Renaissance." *Modern Irish Literature*. Edited by R. J. Porter and J. D. Brophy. New York: 1972, pp. 95–114.

Dunleavy, Janet E. and Gareth W. "Editor Moore to Playwright Hyde: On the Making of *The Tinker and the Fairy*." *Irish University Review* (Spring, 1973), pp. 17–30.

Greene, David. "Synge in the West of Ireland." *Mosaic 5:* 1–8.

Greene, David. "The Founding of the Gaelic League." *The Gaelic League Idea*. Edited by Seán ó Tuama. Cork, 1972.

Murphy, Gerard. "Douglas Hyde 1860–1949." *Studies* 38 (1949): 275—81.

O Dálaigh, Doiminic. "The Young Douglas Hyde." *Studia Hibernica* 10 (1970): 108–35.

O'Hegarty, P. S. *A Bibliography of Dr. Douglas Hyde*. Dublin: 1939.